THE WAY OF THE GODDESS

THE WAY OF THE GODDESS

A Personal Journey of Awakening

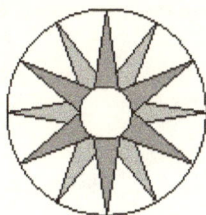

SHANTARA MU KHALSA

Published By
Books of Light Publishing
Colorado, USA

Thanks for all those who helped in the proof reading.
Drawing on pages 92, 202, front cover by Barbara Pines.
Drawing on page 136, front cover reproduction by Lianna Hardy.
Photos on pages 158, 178, 186, back cover by Devani.
Miscellaneous photos, drawings and computer art by Virochana Khalsa.

First Edition 1993
Second Edition 2013
Published by Books of Light Publishing PO BOX 747 Crestone, CO USA
Printed in the United States of America by Lightning Source
Set by Virochana Khalsa in New Times Roman 11 at 14

ISBN 0-9598048-3-8

CONTENTS

To The Eternal One
MAHA AVATAR BABAJI

Through your LOVE I have seen all this world has to offer.

I have seen the gain I have seen the pain

I have seen the mind at play in all its fantastic and extreme ways.

People impoverished, people in need,
people with powers and their castles of worship...

Desires unfulfilled that can never be satisfied -
and the drama that always asks for more...

You have guided me through giving me free rein -
to see and hear and find the way home...

With your Grace I was guided with you at the core -
to allow me to feel the source of creation,
the source of Truth at all times...

I see the perfection in all of this Leela and awake I stand all
One with You - Mother/Father eternal Beloved...

You have given me all I have ever needed to awaken the
perfection within myself.

True Happiness abounds without reason

Nothing to gain and nothing to lose...

Empty and full; at peace with all of creation, I am and
always have been One with Oneness. One with your
Grace...

For you are the One the Mother Serves

She exists because of Your Love, Your Wisdom...

No words can ever express all that is known..

You are the giver and taker of breath, of life and death
and everything stands as a result of Your Love...

There is no more coming or going for this One.

Forever Yours
Forever "ONE..."
SHANTARA MU ...

Sept. 15, 1991

Chapter One

EARLY AWARENESS

This book comes as a result of two occurrences. Firstly it is the result of a personal quest into fulfillment. Secondly it has occurred because of the Grace of the Mother[1] whom I serve.

In places this book may appear to be fantasy-like, and in some ways that is how I have lived my life. I have sought the Divine mystery with passion, always holding my "ideal" as being available here in the physical. I have explored with the intention of manifesting the Divine into my daily life, and refused to settle for second best. Through this I have invoked the Beloved consciousness, and have bought forth the "Beloved Relationship," My Eternal Twin Ray.

Even in today's fast materialistic pace, the Divine Magic is still there to be embraced. If one is willing to step outside of social conventions and values with intense burning and dedication to the "Mystery" or "Divine," one will have the inner experiences and the adventures similar to all great mystics throughout time. It is hoped this book shall serve to inspire *"The Lovers of Life."*

The way I call the Way of the Goddess is the ability and the providence to experience life outside religious and hierarchical structure directly under the Divine Radiation. This way is dependent upon trusting your own inherent intuitive power, and being able to listen to the Divine Will and obey what is being asked of oneself.

---

[1] The Mother is Manifest Creation.

Trusting the unknown is trusting the mysterious play of Divine Mother. There is no technique which can be can be taught that will give one this trust. Only the pure experience of throwing oneself into the Divine Current can bring the experience, which is beyond words. To embrace this way is to embrace the Tantra of life. One must realize oneself as no-thing, thus able to become everything.

The everything and the no-thing are not some far off almost unattainable state. It is simply the willingness to hold oneself as 'ONE' with everything - free of the fears and struggle that come with the illusion you are separate - from the omnipotent omnipresent power of GOD.

The way of the Goddess is the path of Self realization which experiences and maintains this Self Realization in the very natural embrace of the feminine principle. The Feminine principle defies form and transcends all techniques. The masculine or solar principle within us all is that which defines and actualizes our identity - and offers the techniques to achieve certain realization. It is the known - as opposed to the feminine, The way of the Goddess, which is the unknown - The Mystery.

This is generally natural to woman, and as I am embodied as a woman and very emotional, it was the most natural course for my spiritual awakening and the obvious title for my life's story.

It is necessary to understand the totality of the sacrifice, and the intensity which is inevitable, for those entering into the path of Self Liberation. A paradox though it is, our naturally Divine state has become a conditional state of imposed accepted limitations and ignorance of the Divine magic. These limitations and ignorance are what must be removed. For this reason I am required to reveal the personal process I have undergone, in the hope it will be of some value to all travelling this Path.

My journey was always about discovering mySelf as Love and totally understanding That Love.

A sense of freedom has always been natural to me, and from birth I was blessed with a strong will balanced with extreme sensitivity, with the ability to express through dance, play and sports. Happiness was inherent in me, yet I remember being very young, and feeling the lack of free expression in the people around me, and feeling alienated by aspects of adult behavior. My mother tells me I was always a loner - and I remember preferring to observe people rather than participate in group activities.

My family upbringing in a middle class "safe" environment was relatively trauma-free, and I was blessed with loving good parents, an older brother and younger sister, all of whom are still alive. I maintained throughout childhood a secretive communion with nature, and with an unspeakable force, which I could not communicate about with anyone. There is a strong memory of sitting on a beach and talking to the stars knowing I had a home "out there," but no-one ever talked about where they had been before birth. I always knew I had 'been' before.

At the age of sixteen I left school with no intention of entering into university. I had a burning need to know what life was really about and felt university would minimize my ability to think freely and move outside social conventions. In other words, I felt stifled by the limiting education system. It was also natural to me to understand the "truth" I sought was not contained within studies outside of my own being, that is, studies of a philosophical - theoretical nature. Self experiential awareness has always been my guide.

From the age of sixteen it took me twenty years to totally honor, nurture, and obey my sensitive feminine nature. Our materialistic society based on raping and hoarding the Earth's natural resources and dominating less aggressive people is a male dominated one. We can see all too clearly where it is leading.

I was not given an opportunity to feel my femininity as a child in our male dominated society and it forced my competitive side to become more noticeable through sport and feeling the constant pressure to excel intellectually. Women who do not express their passive, intuitive deep feeling natures, are women in pain. Men who never come to peace with their inner women are in pain.

In a state of seeking and rebelling during my late teens, I experimented over a period of two years with marijuana. It was an escape from mundane social consciousness and an exploration into a reality different from that expressed by my parents and society. These experiences alienated me from main stream thinking and awakened in me a greater thirst for finding out who "I" really was. Long term usage of marijuana is very unbalancing and harmful for the body-mind. It creates a non-caring unbalanced laziness, as it dislocates the pineal center in the head. It takes a number of years to regain the clarity of mind that is disrupted by this drug.

Because of this rebelliousness and searching which is at times like being at sea in a small boat without a rudder, I made certain choices not for my highest good. I became pregnant the first two times I was with men sexually with a duration of six months between them. I had two abortions as a result of this - A rather traumatic experience especially the first one, as it was performed in Mexico under poor conditions. This was a confusing time for me adding to an already confused state of not being Self Realized.

Whatever experience we have gives some flavor to us as individuals, and hopefully we grow into happy wise mature beings. I have no particular general advice to young women on this subject of abortion. Each of us will choose to some degree or other certain karmic participation, until through the Grace of a true Teacher, the blessings of timing, and purification by spiritual disciplines we are free of Karmas.

At the age of nineteen, following my two abortions, I contacted a woman who was to be my first inspiration on the spiritual path. This sister's name was Robin. She had just returned to New Zealand from the Sri Aurobindo Ashram in India where she had been living for two years with her seven year old son, Nicholas, studying meditation under her spiritual teachers, The Mother and Sri Aurobindo.

Robin always wore a sari, sandaled feet, and was somebody who had totally stepped outside convention. She was the first person whom I had met who spoke of things that I was needing to hear. Because of my spiritual thirst she embraced me and invited me to live in her house with her. Her husband, an Englishman, was living in quarters at the back of the house, and owned a night club. I met Robin at his club as I would go there to dance regularly. My dancing was an indulgence in my form of self expression, and gave me a creative outlet.

Robin would sit long hours into the night in meditation, write beautiful poetry to the Mother and Aurobindo, and draw mandalas. I remember sitting silently with her and loving her extreme gentleness. This contact was very healing for me, more than I realized at the time.

Robin was having difficulty getting her husband to accept what she was doing, and to accept the fact that she wanted her son, their son, to be brought up in a spiritual environment. He was wanting his son to be with him in his environment which included marijuana and alcohol. Robin was experiencing a lot of pain at this time. One night when we were both in the club, she went into her husband's office in the back and it was obvious that they were in some really heavy discussion as I could see that Robin was crying. I left to go home on my own. The next morning her husband came into the house and informed me that Robin had gone, that she had died. She had left the club about three o'clock in the morning, obviously very distressed, and went outside and sat on the pavement in meditation and consciously left her body.

What always surprised me was that he never seemed to show any remorse, or any emotion about this. I felt that I had lost somebody very precious, and missed her a lot.

I remember grieving, asking myself why did she have to go? Why did she have to leave like that? Now I understand that her pain was so great that she could no longer remain on the planet. About a week after she had died, she came to me in a dream, and gave me a pair of her sandals, and said to me, "your sandaled feet will guide you."

This put my mind at rest, knowing that Robin had never gone, that there was a part of her that was still with me. I left that town shortly after this experience still searching for myself.

Shortly before my twenty-first birthday I incurred an "accident" which had great impact on my life. Whilst having a race on horseback, the horse stumbled in a hole in the ground and I fell. The horse hoof hit and broke my right ankle. The ankle was set crooked and I have had an ankle which is limited in movement ever since. At the time it happened I was very upset and resentful, for I was severely restricted in my movement.

I have come to understand the lesson and "perfection" of this fall. It slowed me down as I had a tendency to "do" more than I needed. It turned my energy inward so that I would take more time to look at what I was doing and creating. It was necessary for me to slow down and gain wisdom before acting impulsively as was my habit. The pain I have had to accept has strengthened my compassion for others. The man I was racing with was very much wanting to show his dominance - and I always needed to challenge this priestly behavior. At that time I was given a harsh lesson about taking on more than I could handle.

I believe this bodily limitation will be completely erased in time. It is gradually being realigned through martial art stances, and the timing of the Collective Light Body being created on earth by those of us committed to awakening. As this "One Christed" body is manifest I am feeling more supported and able to move more confidently on the earth.

It is a great learning to understand how we co-create events such as accidents, disease, miracles, good luck, etc. Through this understanding we can learn how to re-create our limitations and accept what needs acceptance. As we become more conscious we release karmas and we co-create our daily events in a more loving way. In these co-creations I give the last word to the mysterious mastery or "perfection" of the <u>Uni</u>verse and remain at peace as everything is manifest.

When I was twenty-three I took LSD three times and woke up! I saw the omnipresent lifeforce in all of nature and realized that much was to be understood through activating more of the brain. The third time I took it "GOD" told me not to take any more. I vomited the drug up in response to this command and have never taken it since. After seven years of Yogic practices I took cobra venom once, and one year later ate hallucinogenic mushrooms twice, and several years later took the hallucinogenic drug Ecstasy three times. In all these later experiments I could watch what they were doing to my metabolism and choose to go with it - or override it. I never lost control and used it as a meditation.

I have found no drug to be a worthy substitute for stabilized transformative spiritual disciplines, far from it in fact. Nothing can give us ongoing enlightenment in a pure way other than our own supreme application of Self realization practices, along with the mysterious force of Divine Grace of the "ONE." Therefore I believe psychedelic drugs are harmful and should be avoided. The pure experience of Love Bliss gained through devotional practice is a far greater intoxication - and one which can lead a person into greater Self Realization.

At this time, whilst under the influence of my third LSD experience, I had become pregnant. It is still a mystery as I was not sexually involved with my companion (or ever was). I wished to be a healthy mother, one that was of value to the incoming child. It was then that I moved away from my known city environment into a rural community, that was based on the organic growing of food. Here I became a vegetarian, which was quite unusual in New Zealand in the early seventies. I lived in one of the primitive structures alone, and made my peace with the earth and healed my body from the pollutive input of the city and drugs.

Here for the first time, I experienced and participated in cutting wood for cooking over a wood stove, heating my home in this way, chopping wood daily, and bathing either in the outdoor flowing stream or in an outdoor bath. We would light a fire underneath the bath, often towards sunset, and bath in it under the evening stars and breeze amongst the trees. This was all very healing, very nurturing. I also dug outdoor holes in the ground for toilets, and, which gives a complete new way of relating to the earth, using our own waste for nutrients within the soil. Water was collected from the roof, and there was no dependence on the electricity and water supplies, and conveniences which one usually experiences in city living.

Living in this way, one's life automatically slows into a natural rhythm of interaction and participation with the earth, and there is a tremendously healing force and impact upon the body to wake up in the morning, to walk into the garden to pick the fruits and vegetables for the day. This gave me a sense of total connectivity and respect and gratitude for all that comes from the Earth.

I spent approximately three hours every day in the garden participating in the growing of these foods, and watching how the earth and how the forces of nature provide constantly for the well being of mankind. This tremendous teaching brought great peace to my inner being.

I really loved walking in the rain, lying on the earth, in the sun, gardening in the sun, and spending so much of my time alone in direct relationship with the elements. This was always a great joy for me, and always will be.

In this home I read a few spiritual books which had a profound impact on me, and my inner journey of yoga and meditation began. A prayer arose from within me, and through dreams I became awoken to the reality that somebody, something was listening to those prayers: for there was always a response.

During my pregnancy I had my first conscious interaction with a Realized being on the inner. A well known Yogi, Swami

Venkatesananda - who has since left the earth, came into my dream. In the dream I had cycled to his abode and entered. He looked at me lovingly and said "what are you doing here - You know what you have to do." I continued practising daily Hatha yoga and silent meditation. It is true to say that during much of my life I have had the feeling of living on a mountain top, as I have a strong ability to feel unattached to much of life's petty occurrences. In the last few years I have come to fully understand why I had these strong detachments, that my most recent lifetimes and others were lived as a yogini under a Master's guidance.

Shortly after my first dream teachings, I had another dream transmission. I walked up a staircase of white light and met a being in a Golden Light at the top. He handed me a large golden key and said "Your son is the beginning of a revolution."

This was a blessing from the Beloved Ascended Master Koothumi, who is known in the Great White Brotherhood as Lord of the Golden Ray. This realization of the Master's name came to me thirteen years later. He was also known as Guru Ram Dass of the Sikh Gurus, Saint Francis of Assisi, and Quetzecoatyl a Mayan ruler.

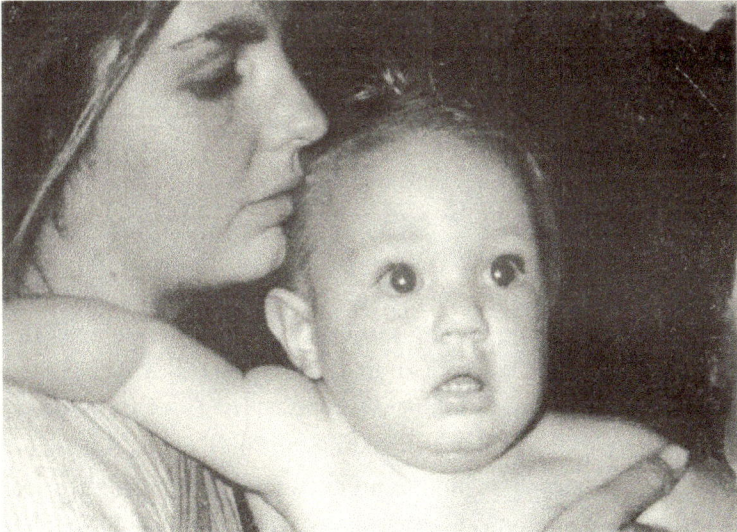

I have come to understand the message of Koothumi. My son heralded into the Earth the deified[2] energy of Subramuniya, "He who leads the legions of angels." He is also one of the fallen angels of the being "Osiris," and has come now to help bring back the parts of Osiris into a whole relationship with the Earth. This healing will release much collective karma and liberate great potential upon the planet, in which the Osiris energy plays a major part.

In truth we are all angelic beings, and most of us have fallen from the "LIGHT OF GRACE." Recently my Beloved and I have been shown how the energy of Osiris - a god of Egypt - was a soul with a highly developed mental body.

This group soul upon incarnating into physicality believed it could do things "better" and stepped out of the ordained Earth's timing of evolutionary development for the collective soul process. In this downward rebellion this collective soul group called "Osiris" captured various siddhic powers from the inner-world (forth and fifth dimensions) and created the doorway for these limited elemental psychic powers to become fused into the subconscious fabric of humankind. This was the beginning of "shamanism," the worshipping of powers and the animalistic forms representing those powers. This created the ability for a few who could master these powers to control the masses, who had lost their belief in the inner "Light" of Love.

Now is the programmed timing for these karmas to be released from the Earth's karmic cellular memory and the "Osiris" soul group is assisting the earth with the process - though mostly semi-consciously.

This is the time on Earth now - that the light is overcoming the darkness, and the souls of ONENESS are waking up. This is also known as the re-activation of the Crystal Grid, The Golden Age, and the birthing of the Collective Christ Body (also known as the Body of the "Khalsa" meaning the "pure of Heart").

When I was six months pregnant, I knew I was to be moved on from the community. At that time I wrote to a lady I had met a

---

[2] A deified form is an embodiment carrying an energy that is acknowledged as holding certain Divine qualities.

few months earlier asking if there was space for me on their land further north. She had previously extended an invitation to stay whenever it felt appropriate. Her response was affirmative, and I drove my old car, which went by Grace, to a beautiful area of the North of New Zealand. The land was over a harbor inlet, with deep calm blue water and trees down to the water line. These friends had a barge they lived on, and graciously gave me a cabin on the land to myself. It was a happy time and I was at peace. My meditations continued and I was also inwardly asking for a spiritual guide.

One sunny peace filled morning a man walked down the hill onto the property and I met him on the track. Instantly I knew he was the answer to my prayer for a guide. It seems he knew straight away also. For after a few minutes he looked at me and said "I have been sent from India to help you."

This was a shock to Richard, as he had been in New Zealand only a few weeks and did not want to be settled anywhere in particular. He left saying he would return - and I went into quietude. Two days later he came again and said "let us go and find a home we can both live in."

This instant friend had just spent two years in India living as a Sadhu with yogis, and was very committed to his Self realization. He was an American from Hawaii.

We got on well. It was mostly a non verbal relationship - both of us preferring peace, quiet, and meditation. We rented an old Kauri wood farm house - spacious, sunny and in a setting with large trees, established garden, and a stream running through the backyard. Very pleasant.

My pregnancy was for me a wonderful experience. I gained good health, a sense of inner peace, and looked forward to being a mother. When it came time for me to give birth to my son, I had hoped it could occur in the house where we were living. However at that time home births were fairly rare and not encouraged so to speak by the medical profession. I had seen a doctor only twice during my pregnancy, at the beginning and again towards the end, never feeling that it was necessary for I always knew that I was doing well.

The doctor in the local area had agreed that because the woman who owned the farmhouse, the farmer's wife, was a nurse and lived close by, that if it was my choice she could assist at the birth at home. My mother arrived for a visit and was there on the evening that I went into labor. She had little confidence in me having this child at home and after a couple of hours of labor, unknown to me, went across the road and called the ambulance to take me into hospital.

When the ambulance arrived the doctor came in and said that the child was upside down and that it was going to be a long hard birth. Having no previous experience, I could do little except trust what he was saying and surrender to their wishes. On the way into the ambulance I said I felt that the child was almost there and would have preferred to stay at home, yet they did not listen. In the ambulance I said I felt my waters had broken and that it was very close, again they did not listen.

Fifteen minutes later we got into the hospital, they put me on a bed and realized that the child was almost out. If I had not been interrupted in my labor process it would have been a very easy birth. The child came out very easily and it was an experience that would have been much more beneficial to me and my son had we been in our quiet peaceful home environment instead of doctors and nurses running around, lights flashing and an atmosphere that I found to be rather gross.

Richard had managed to come into the delivery room with me and was playing his flute happily. After the birth of my healthy son whom Richard named Sunjaya I lay down in the hospital bed and went to sleep for a couple of hours. Waking, I found a plate of mince beside me, instantly vomited, and asked to leave the hospital. The nurse seemed to have little understanding that I would have vomited at the sight of wakening to mincemeat. It was obvious that I was in the wrong place. After signing papers releasing the hospital from all responsibility should anything go wrong, I happily bundled up my child and took him home, after a duration of six hours in the hospital. From then on it was a very joyous experience for me and being a mother was always very natural.

As has always been the case in my life Divine providence was playing out and Richard decided after a couple of weeks he would return to Hawaii to tend to some business there and make a decision as to whether we should continue in a relationship and for him to take on the responsibility of being a father, meaning our relationship would therefore become more intimate. I decided to take my child at this time down to my family home 500 miles away.

Whilst we were away from the farmhouse the farmer attending the house saw some marijuana plants which Richard had growing in the back of the house which he had for his personal use. I must say that at no time did I really feel Richard was in any way using marijuana in an abusive manner, in fact I remember only ever seeing him smoking twice in three months. For some reason he felt he still needed it and at that time I had not the depth of wisdom to see certain underlying issues in him.

The farmer chose to call the police and when I returned to the farmhouse, just before the return of my friend from Hawaii, they told me they would be meeting him upon his arrival back into the country. Richard had been back in the house only a few hours having told me that he would stay with us when the police walked in and arrested him. He was sentenced to deportation and I saw him again only once when I visited him in the penitentiary where he was held before being put on an aeroplane.

I was quite shocked by this whole occurrence yet always inside of me has been a trust of the play of the universe, and I released that experience within a few months. I did however develop a gastric stomach for a few weeks due to the stress of this relationship terminating so abruptly and feeling the aloneness and responsibility of being a solo mother. I was assisted by some friends who helped me change my diet further and allowed me to relax into motherhood by being in the house with me for a few days and assist in the care of my child.

About three months after the birth of my son I knew that I needed a spiritual teacher in the physical, and trusted the Divine would respond to my call. Knowing this, I followed my guidance to leave the farmhouse where I was staying, and to go to the community where I had been before my pregnancy to wait for the physical teacher to come to me. Here again I remained alone in one of the primitive structures and settled into enjoying being a mother gaining the confidence that was necessary in being blessed with a very healthy and happy child.

Two years ago my Beloved and I were shown in a few dreams how Richard had come into my life from a past life experience in Egypt. At that time he was one of the priests who plotted to have my child killed (who consequently is my son again in this lifetime.)

It was ordained by providence that he have connection with both my son and I at this time. It is interesting to note that simultaneously two years ago just before we were shown the dreams, Richard had gone to great lengths to find out where I was and had rang my father in New Zealand asking that I contact him. Doing so he said he had been feeling strongly that he needed to reconnect with my Sunjaya. At that time we were shown the dreams and I contacted him again letting him know the karmic reasons for this interaction, and how it could be completed most graciously. He declined to follow through and went into a great rage, refusing even the possibility that what I was saying was truth.

This was a completion of this interaction, and for a few days we felt the psychic kickback of this energy not yet willing to see a part of itself that has perpetuated the priestly karma.

By the time Sunjaya was eight months old I met my first teacher, who reinforced the reality that I had a strong spiritual destiny, which was already cut and woven. All I needed to do was stay open and continue a greater commitment to specific practices, which I did. These were Meditation, Pranayama[3], and Hatha Yoga[4], and living a contemplative existence in pure environments close to the Mother. When Sunjaya was fourteen months, we went to live in an Ashram to be with people of a like mind. Within four months a Swami from India came and I listened to him.

---

[3] Pranayama - conscious application of breath to invoke increased lifeforce in the body.

[4] Hatha Yoga - Hatha literally translates from Sanskrit meaning strength. More commonly known as a practice to create a flexible and at- ease body, using slow movement, still postures, and focused breathing techniques.

Chapter Two

JOURNEYS IN INDIA AND SPIRITUAL LESSONS

*A*s the swami talked of surrender to the Guru, I felt this was what I was looking for. His teacher who had never been out of India had sent him specifically to get me. This he later told me. There was no doubt in my mind that I would go to India to forward my spiritual journey. A devotional trusting attitude was very natural to me and surrender came easily to the teacher and to the instructions that were given. This surrender is the inherent nature of the feminine principle.

The burning desire for me to become One with Love (God) was a flame greater than any thing else in my life. This is the intensity that is necessary for any soul who wants to find "GOD" to succeed. There was an excitement and anxiety in the realization that now my whole life was going to change dramatically. I hoped all the time that I could travel with Sunjaya to India, but it became apparent that I would have to leave alone, and that "my last remaining at-

tachment" was undergoing a test, to be "given up," so to speak.

This was the most difficult things I have ever done, or will ever do. One who is truly a mother understands the depths of bonding that there is between a mother and a greatly loved child. There was a force that overtook my moments of weakness which I could only describe as coming from a part of mySelf that I had not yet consciously realized. This force allowed me to go through the pain filled actions of letting go of my son into the hands of some very supportive friends before travelling to India, for my stay of nine months. This action was a completion to break attachment to any form. Since that time I have always been able to move when necessary, without attachment to any form or image or personality. By the time I left for India Sunjaya was two years of age.

Upon my arrival in India, the Mother embraced me as I put my feet on the soil. I felt a coming home, in a way that I had never felt on the Earth before, and I lay down and kissed the ground. It was obvious that some of my incarnations were deeply rooted into that culture. There is a natural alignment within me to the spiritual currents, of that ancient culture, a deeply surrendered and more accepting state of being. Even today parts of India exist without the materialistic striving

and stresses that burden our western society. The slowness of the pace of life creates the space for a more introspective existence.

Whilst travelling to the Master in the countryside of Uttar-Pradesh, I was embraced in a different reality. Leaving time as I had known it before, I arrived in a bullock drawn cart, which was the only transport available for the final fifteen miles.

The Love that greeted me through The Master upon my arrival was overpowering to such a degree, that within twenty-four hours I had a very high fever. This fever was the purifying effect of my complete surrender. It was the burning out of all present life Karmas (impurities) that were held in my aura. This all-consuming fever was is known as the awakening of the Kundalini[1] which for me was transmitted through the penetrating glance of the Master whom I saw as Krishna[2] personified. All resistance to the Divine Will was burned out. All images that I had as an individual personality (ego) were by Divine Grace burned out. This was for me a totally ecstatic death, and even the thought of dying or not dying did not arise as "I" was consumed in the fire of Love, blending with the master. This awakening into Love Bliss is the doorway into the Divine realms, and is looked upon as a high achievement on the spiritual path. At this point all sense of "my will" was obliterated. My mind remained completely dissolved during the next nine months in India. Throughout this period I regularly needed caring for by the way of food being prepared, and clothes being washed, as I had lost all desire to care for my body. It was a miracle of Grace.

The ordained relationship, from previous incarnations with the Master, was for me to be his tantric consort as well as devotee. Through physical intimacy in which no words were verbalized I was graced with the ongoing deepening of Love Bliss and much awakening. A relationship of this status is in no way like any worldly desire-filled association. It is pure red Tantra and is a great blessing, earned by a soul who has given up the ego, into the Love of

---

[1] Kundalini - the manifesting and energetic power of consciousness.

[2] Krishna - a Hindu God personifying Divine Love. The Eternal Master BabaJi was the actual incarnation of Krishna around 5,000 years ago. BabaJi is presently living in an eternal body in the Himalayas, which he has maintained for thousands of years.

the Divine. Through sanskara, pure longing, and Divine timing, a Master appears who is the Realized form of Divine Love.

I believe this blessed relationship is established in many lifetimes of practising spiritual disciplines, and at the "right time," one is re-initiated into the true understanding of Self and the purpose of life. My tantric relationship was a totally sacred transmission[3] which I had been prepared for.

Even though I had no language at that time to express my knowledge, my heart understood the great gift I was being given freely. It was in fact an added blessing that I have never approached my spiritual journey from an intellectual viewpoint, which always needs to know what is going on. This very wanting to know, often stops spontaneous experience of the Divine.

Pure Love, is death. Everyone must at some point come to the mature spiritual understanding that Love is just that.

One cannot control Love, one cannot demand Love. Love comes and is given freely, as the Divine agency Wills. The form is not to be caught in, and should remain the secondary focus.

Love is from the formless pure radiant Self, which we all are in truth. It is in fact Relationship with that Self which we already are, and we are just Loving ourSelf through another form, who is in truth also us.

Such a play, such a joy, such a death, to die, to need, to possess another, as our source of Bliss and happiness. A true tantric master awakens the knowingness of the Oneness into the very cells of another, and is able to purify any layers of (karma) separation.

Tears of relief and joy became a part of my everyday existence

[3] Sacred Transmission - the grace of the Oneness which reveals the inner mysteries and transforms the aspirant. Can come through a Spiritual teacher's physical presence. As a spiritual aspirant's mind becomes more aligned in the Oneness these transmissions are able to be received consciously through the inner planes (Enlightened dream state).

during this nine months under the protection of this Master. There was very little speaking during this whole time, as he normally did not speak English, and I did not speak or even wish to learn Hindi.

I realized that he was allowing me to totally embrace Him without entering into a dependent dualistic relationship. It was an added wisdom at this time also, not to enter into discussion with the many other devotees.

Obvious gossiping and petty disagreements were demonstrated by the large numbers of devotees around this Master. They demonstrated their own lack of practise and surrender by displaying such behavior. Fortunately by not speaking the language, I was saved from these impurities landing on my ears.

It is advised to all seekers not to get caught up in organizational social traps of power and pettiness on your spiritual journey! I have yet to observe a group of "followers" where this does not occur. It is as One may say "The Nature of the Beast of Duality."

Devotion moved through my being at this time with ecstatic songs, tears and dance. I learned to play the Harmonium, an Indian keyboard instrument, and daily, devotees played music and sang Kirtan[4]. The Master was also a great singer and played drums and the harmonium. Love Bliss was my outward and inward state.

The Master was a householder, with children and grandchildren. His wife would come and wash his feet and put flowers around my neck after the time we shared tantrically. This act of pure Love on her part gave me a great teaching in the nature of true relationship with enlightened beings. I used this experience as a powerful guideline on the absolute allowance and freedom that comes with Love. These transcended[5] beings - (the Master and his wife) - radiated grace, dignity, and joy at all times.

This experience was my transformation, and paved the way for greater enlightenment.

During this time I often had high temperatures, partly caused by the lack of fresh green foods, and organic grains, that I

---

[4] Kirtan - Devotional Singing.

[5] Transcended - Self Realized state to move beyond limitation.

had been used to. I ate many sweets which Hindus call Prasad, and there was lack of clean fresh water for drinking and bathing.

There was nothing in my comfortable upbringing in New Zealand that could have prepared me for the culture shock I experienced at the poverty in India. The earth in so many places seemed harsh and ungiving. I was used to much physical space, lush green abundance of nature's gifts and pure abundance of flowing clean water.

This dry dusty harshness of the environment and poverty level of too many people in one area scratching out a subsistence life style because there was no choice, added to my nausea and sickness.

My body suffered from this, along with the tremendous heat which I had never experienced before. The Master would come on occasions when I was lying on my bed and lovingly place his hand on my forehead. I felt at the time this loving touch increased the fever through his purifying touch. He would always come as a response to my inner call for him.

One hot sunny still afternoon I walked about a half kilometer outside of the Ashram compound to sit under some trees by a pond. About twenty minutes later, as I was sitting in meditation I became aware of voices calling in the background, but did not feel like responding. Shortly later I opened my eyes to see two or three snakes crawling in a circle around myself and the tree. One stood on its back, opened its hood, and looked at me. I knew it was a cobra - yet it never occurred to me to feel scared or even bother to move. It was my first encounter with snakes, as there are none in New Zealand. Somehow I felt blessed to be close to wild creatures who seemed to be meditating with me. They continued circling around me for about another half hour.

After an hour I returned to the compound as was told not to go to that area as snakes lived there. I smiled and said "yes, I have already met them." Years later I had remembrance of a past embodiment in Greece where I saw myself resting with Cobra snakes next to me. These creatures I believe have helped to protect temples, priests, and priestesses in the past. My reconnecting with them again was easy and one of safe familiarity. This was also the blessings of the "Mother" coming forth.

The Swami who brought me from New Zealand became jealous of my intimacy with the Master. The Swami and I with several other devotees went to the Swami's Ashram when the Master travelled out from his home. We stayed in the Ashram in Vrindaban for one month. Vrindaban is known as the abode of Krishna the God of Divine Love. I continued to experience and express a bliss filled absorption in the Love of the Divine and the transmissions I had received continued to be received on an etheric level.

The Swami who had been asked to care for me, was supposedly celibate, now outwardly displayed his jealousy. Understanding that I had a physical tantric relationship with his master, he proposed a similar relationship with me. I refused and our relationship deteriorated. One day when he had taken me for a few days alone to New Delhi his jealousy turned to anger, and because he could not control me in the way he had wanted to, he lashed out, hit me in the face, and cracked my jaw with his ring. I had to go for dental treatment to have my jaw wired, and could take no food for a number of weeks, just sipping liquids through a straw.

When we returned to the Master in Uttar Pradesh, he was very disturbed by the incident. He was very caring as to the correct treatment that I should receive, and made certain that I had fresh vegetable juice every day so that my strength would return. After a couple of weeks the Master asked of me to go with the Swami to England and Europe for his first visit, to assist him in establishing and disseminating this teaching. I said I would go, because the Master had requested it.

In England I was very unhappy. We stayed in London for a few weeks; it was a cold, dreary, noisy city, and also I no longer related to the Swami in a heartfelt way. I did not like the Swami propagating himself, and could see that I was being groomed for a position which would be for me a hypocrisy. Whilst we were in Germany, I told him I wanted to return to New Zealand; I had received news that Sunjaya had been ill, and was fretting for my attention. I received the Master's blessings from India to do so and eleven months after leaving Sunjaya and New Zealand, I returned.

This Swami is now set up internationally with a very large following and continues to attract people who are willing to have this limited experience.

Having Realized the Divine as my eternal consort and that no separation from this union was possible, I knew I would get stronger by daily maturing my awareness. Maya (illusion) is the arising of desires that entrenches One in duality, seeking external security - approval - image - comfort. When our attention is drawn away from the 'Oneness' and the perfect knowingness of "being as the ONE" we enter into dualistic awareness - This leads to desires, feeling lack, judgement, and creating semiconscious incomplete actions called Karmas. Once in the realm of karmas we come under the power of what is called Maya (illusion). It is my experience, that the only desire that leads to true happiness is the desire to be One with Love, (God). This looks like desirelessness and that is what it is. This is what I call true Yoga, "the Yoga of necessity to become enlightened." My way has been to experience what has been given to me, asked of me, shown to me, without desire; to perform action as though it is the Lord performing through me. This finally leads to the realization of "I AM GOD IN ACTION."

Upon leaving India I was ten kilograms lighter from the intense purification of my kundalini rising. I was extremely happy to be reunited with Sunjaya, who was almost three years of age by now. We lived for some months on 600 acres of native bush and trees in an isolated vegetarian community on the Coromandel pennisula of New Zealand. I lived with the Divine through communion with nature and preferred the sounds of the river, wind, and birds. During this time there was just the experience of communion. Communion I call common-union, it was always there. At that time I called it Krishna.

The experience I had been through in India had left me less able to fit into society. No longer the person that had left for India - I needed time to integrate that transformation more, and enjoyed being alone with Sunjaya. To others it appeared that I was disconnected, maybe brainwashed - which of course in a sense was true. We are from childhood imprinted and impacted by the realities of those nearest to us and the values of society into which we have been born. I chose to seek another set of values and find a new identity. This I had achieved, though I could not comfortably express its transforming benefits. In India I had felt recognized for whom I really was, a devoted consort of the Divine, and had been protected by the Satsang (Divine association) of my Master and devotees.

It was difficult for me to communicate to others as they had no reality of what I was experiencing. As a mother I enjoyed my child immensely, but there was judgement upon the way I was living from those who did not understand, including my family.

To speak of this is important, for everyone must understand what will be faced in awakening true spiritual life and going against social conventions. There were many tears on my part during the next few years of ordeal, as those closest to me seemed far away, yet my determination to find my true Self remained, and kept me going.

It became obvious that Sunjaya needed more interaction with other children, so we left our peace-filled simple home and moved to a city where he could attend preschool, three times weekly. This he enjoyed for he is naturally outgoing and sociable.

Within a month, I found a group of devotees who were practising other forms of meditation. It felt right for me to continue experiencing, and expand my understanding of various Yogic practices.

The success of spiritual life for me ultimately comes down to success in relationship. Self absorption at times is necessary to purify and strengthen One's Sadhana[6]. Then the initiate will need to give to others the fruits of their practise, however this seems most wisely appropriate, and this "emptying" out nourishes the One Self. In this way we do not recoil from life, instead we continue to grow more wise by consciously participating in life and awakening to our fullest potential.

---

[6] Sadhana - any conscious practice which assists in the development and awakening of a Soul into it Self.

Chapter Three

MORE SPIRITUAL JOURNEYS

Some of these new forms of meditation were physically very dynamic, and there was also chanting[1] and silence. I had been in such a dissolved state, it was strengthening for me to reconnect to my body awareness again. This inherent sense of balance has been a strong indicator throughout my journey, as I passed different stages of initiations[2] and Realized all initiations need to be tested in daily life.

As we grow spiritually we are automatically raising our vibration, and finishing with karmas of a more dense or gross level. For me this journey began with leaving behind drugs, meat, coarse people and unclear relationships. Speaking truth, standing in the light of what we believe, and a wish to align with the ONENESS, are all absolutely vital steps up the ladder towards freedom and happiness.

I have found as I progress up this ladder that life has become more and more graceful and joyous. In the early stages the ego fears the illusion of death, fears the feelings of dying, and hangs on to the "known." These feelings of separation must die to be truly reborn in the "ONENESS."

---

[1] Mantra (chanting) - focussed harmonized repetition of sounds and feeling to assist a person in awakening their essence qualities.

[2] Initiations - the introductory experience to a newly discovered reality.

I believe that not until mankind acknowledges spiritually enlightened leaders of the ONENESS as their true leaders will we have peace on earth. The chosen leadership planetarily reflects the accepted standards of greed, selfishness, ignorance, and corruption. It will take major natural planetary disturbances before most are willing to change their ways. Being unwilling to participate in these levels of karmas - and in truth not needing to perpetuate these karmas - I have never involved myself in social activities such as school committees, social rights groups, political marches, and band wagons or even voting. In New Zealand there was one elected Prime Minister whom I was shown in the inner had been close to me in Atlantis and was a very evolved soul. He helped this country become Nuclear Free and this was a great thing considering the state of Worldly misaffairs. I wrote him an inspired letter which he answered. That is the extent of my political leanings.

I believe the inherent strength of the Goddess at one with the Mother is her ability to stay close to and resonate with the Earth's needs. This has always been important to me.

We as a humanity have immersed our identity in separation (illusion) and created suffering and unhappiness. All the beauty, freedom and heaven we are seeking is around us and in us with every conscious breath, flowing through the Grace of the Mother as she unfolds her secrets willingly. All we need to do is reach out, relax, and reclaim that kingdom.

I enjoyed the daily discipline and increased vitality gained in these new practices, and enjoyed the company of new friends. The Mystery enticed me and I was still a devotee. I knew the experience of the Divine, but had not yet fully Realized mySelf as the Divine.

In this devotional stage of the Self Realized process the upper chakras[3] are beginning to be activated more completely.

---

[3] Chakras - an energy vortex which assists manifestation to become more conscious of its totality. Traditionally there are seven main chakra centers in the spinal cord of the human body. In reality chakras exist in all forms of creation. They assist in the transmutation of energy by quickening molecular existence in the Oneness. Ultimately only one chakra exists, when there is no distinction of separation.

The heart chakra is opened to the Divine in all existence. Until this devotion is awoken, a person remains in the drama of the first three chakras, or what another Master calls the first three stages of life. A physical teacher is essential, during these formative stages, to dissolve the egoistic illusions of existence (all the feelings and beliefs of separation).

The unavoidable vulnerability and naivety of a true devotee, can lead to a number of different types of experiences and a novice can for a time be misguided and manipulated by beings holding certain powers for power's sake. These beings I now have come to understand as fifth dimensional teachers and there are many in the world arena of name and fame.

After practising these new forms of meditation for almost one year, I decided to travel to India and be a part of the Ashram in Poona. There was a community growing rapidly around this new teacher, and I wanted to put my son into a school that taught basic spiritual awareness through yoga and meditation. I arrived in the Ashram and within three days it was obvious that there was much going on that Sunjaya (now four years of age) and I could not be a part of. It was one of my experiences within this field of the fifth dimensional teachers which I had now encountered on this my second visit to India. I had nowhere else to go, and I decided to "take the best and leave the rest." This motto became very much a part of my vocabulary for a few years.

Here within this Ashram there were many beings wanting power over others to maintain the hierarchy. I have come to realize it was a reflection of all the impurities of the teacher who was being worshipped - Bhagwan Rajneesh. Being one of these teachers of the fifth dimensional realm, still based in separative existence, he enjoyed games of self grandisement, which distorted the spiritual essence which lay underneath some of his teachings. His physical body was reflecting his limited spiritual attainment, though I did not know as much as I do now about diseasement. He had many allergies and was a diabetic, certainly this shows karmic issues not being addressed. This I have come to know fully in these past seven years.

Most of these fifth dimensional teachers involved in the karmas of this level have large followings, for there are many seekers who feel secure in belonging to large structures of a religious nature, and who are not yet ready or able to stand in their own light. Not agreeing with the status quo in this Ashram immediately put me on the outer. I disliked intensely the accepted violent behavior within certain group therapies and the acceptance of drug taking.

The Ashram was more an experimental emotional therapeutic dumping ground, than a place of peace-filled purity and meditation. I saw people with broken bones as the result of others' anger, incurred in therapies!

Rajneesh had a policy of allowing almost every type of person and behavior into his following including drug taking. He maintained a position of aloof worship using his charismatic quality and psychic powers of the magician to hold himself over and above his "followers." I could see how people were cultivating a stance of separation in worshipping this way and I often spoke out against "idolizing" one man.

It is true that overall I needed that experience as it was necessary for my own maturing and understanding that came as a result of this experience. Phenomena[4] also became a more prominent part of my life and I clearly learned that I did not want to be part of the desire for power over others, nor did I intend to be controlled by others.

In this time of my spiritual search, when I felt tremendously alone and unsupported, and still kept going, I was unable to show the depth of my pain. This pain has been stored in parts of my body, such as my lower back and was still coming up for release fourteen years later. The pain of not feeling supported, of being around people who never understood the depths of my sensitivity, the pain of feeling other people's pain, because I could see that they were giving away their power to people to abuse them. The pain of remaining in an unclear situation and feeling helpless. The pain of the feminine principle which has been abused for so long on this planet.

---

[4] Phenomena - the play of duality executed via the Divine Will which most may term "miraculous."

It never was my tendency to doubt myself. I always had trust in my determination and courage to keep going on no matter what; but at this stage of my growth, as a result of this experience, I carried the feeling that I was on the earth plane to suffer, because I felt that so much of humankind was in a state of tremendous destructiveness. I became what I meditated on, and I meditated on the disharmony and I saw the limitations and the pain, and by doing so, I allowed that into my being, because I was not enlightened, and could not at this time overcome all these feelings of opposition, along with the feeling that I had to challenge energies of darkness whenever I saw them. It was a force: I was driven to go into these arenas with these powerful magicians, to challenge these energies, and then to leave them, knowing it was not what I wanted to be a part of.

The heart of all beings is an open book to the Oneness. It is the Mother in all of nature, and all Her awoken forms, that I have always recognized as the temple in which to worship. This of course is the way of the Goddess, no one ultimately above another.

Rajneesh was suffering from his own Karmas. His health was chronically out of balance and he died some seventeen years later. He was at a level which I know now as a fifth dimensional limitation still being fascinated by his power over others.

FEW BEINGS ON THIS EARTH PLANE HAVE TRULY UNDERSTOOD WHAT IT MEANS TO CARRY SPIRITUAL POWER AND HOW IT IS TO BE WISELY USED. These are all necessary experiences for the seeker to pass through, and every school of learning is valuable if one gains some wisdom by it. Fortunately, as I was able and willing to acknowledge the limitations in this Ashram, it was a very short time before I was moved.

This timing came in the form of a profound experience when I was feeling despair. My beloved son had typhoid and almost died. After his recovery, he was returned to New Zealand with my sister-in-law who had come to help us. I was at a loss to know what to do. I had been ill and was very depleted by the psychic battlefield I was in.

During this dark hour of my life, a being who was a jewel from heaven saved Sunjaya's life and gave me much comfort. I was sleeping in the Hospital with my son, who was critically ill. Dr. Vasant Lad, who was the head of the ayurvedic hospital, spiritually recognized me and said that he felt that he had to help me, to repay the kindness I had shown him in a past life. Every night as he finished his rounds he would come and meditate with Sunjaya deep into the night, read him stories, and did everything possible for him. When the illness had reached its peek, Doctor Lad told me that Sunjaya had actually physically died, that he no longer had to be on this earth plane, but that my Love brought him back.

It seemed so harsh that Sunjaya had to go through this pain, and I was crying out to be allowed to take on his pain. Yet the law of life is exact. Sunjaya asked me why he had to have such pain. I said "maybe it is so that you can understand other people's pain from now on in your life." Later, in New Zealand when I was first permitted to see Sunjaya by my brother, I sat with him on the grass, and he put his hand on my head and said "Mummy, I know that I can never die."

I wanted to regain my health before returning to New Zealand. Also I was very aware that I had previously felt betrayed and misunderstood by all my family members in regards to my searching and seeking on the spiritual path. They had no understanding or support for the burning desire of my spiritual quest. Knowing that I would be returning into this lack of understanding and support was a big reason why I chose at this point, a crucial turning point in my life, not to return to New Zealand to be with my son, until I was stronger. My family interpreted this as meaning I was unwilling to be a mother, and my brother went and obtained interim custody of my child, on the grounds that I had deserted him.

I was crying out for deeper understanding one night as I was lying on a bench in the Ashram. I opened my eyes to see a very unusual little man about four feet tall playing in front of me with bottles and string. He was communicating to me through his play, and a group of children came, danced around him and then left. I closed my eyes to receive the understanding of this, and Realized that "life was just a play with no meaning to be sought for." When I opened my eyes a few seconds later the little man had vanished, and I got up to walk out of the Ashram, wondering how he had even got in, as the gates were guarded and only devotees were allowed in at night. As I walked, an all encompassing voice, very loud from within and without, spoke and said, "Where are you going, there is nothing outside of you. I am in you, we are ONE." This was again a lifesaving transmission from Beloved Ascended Master Koothumi. That was what I needed to free myself from this experience and that teacher.

I have since understood that the little man was this particular size because he was from the inner earth - where our collective Oneness is registered and understood.

Totally letting go of this teacher and teaching, I made the decision to go North until I was strong enough to return to Sunjaya. I knew I would be with the Divine wherever I went and trusted totally that what I required would always be with me.

Koothumi Lal Singh
The Ascended Master of the Golden Ray

After leaving the Ashram I travelled towards North India. On my travels at times when I had no place to stay I would find a temple or small Ashram to rest. In these places kindly devotees would always offer adequate food and peace. I was in a state where I neither felt alive nor dead. The Tibetan Buddhists have a word for this, they call it the state of Bhardo, where everything that one has known about oneself becomes dissolved, there is nothing to go back to, and nothing is known of what is ahead.

It was Grace that carried me through these times. Though I always had a tremendous inherent trust of the Divine force that was moving me, I had little trust in the people whom I saw that were engrossed in separative materialistic existence.

I had been invited by an Indian devotee of the Poona Ashram to come and visit him and his family at any time I wished. He was upset with me for taking off my mala and leaving the teachings, yet his love for me continued as a friend. When he and another friend heard that I was travelling, they came by vehicle from their village to an Ashram temple where I was staying, and asked if I would go with them to their village and remain for some time as their guest. I happily accepted their invitation and we went to the village. My friends were wonderful musicians and makers of instruments.

In the village I enjoyed much music and chanting with other devotees. These Indian devotees were poor in the material sense yet rich in the spiritual sense, for their hearts were open and showing great love for the Divine. After a few weeks I knew it was time for me to move on. I left not knowing where to spend the night.

I sat down on the side of the dusty road outside the village and inwardly asked, "what now?" A few minutes later a young servant boy came running across the road from a large home with walls all around the compound. He asked me to come in. When I went inside a pleasant attractive lady greeted me and told me she had been at her bench preparing food when a voice said to her "send your servant out on to the road, you have a guest." This lady remembered seeing me in the village a few days earlier and I was made welcome. We developed a close friendship and I stayed for several weeks. During

this time we shared stories - she wrote very beautiful poetry, and I sewed some new style clothes for the two young children. Here I felt at peace and unhindered. I enjoyed wholesome food and had a much needed rest regaining my strength.

Whilst staying in this house with the family who took me off the road, I remember lying on the roof on the rope bed the Indians make to sleep in at night under the stars. I would go up in the heat of the day, in the blazing sun, and lie on the bed, wishing that I could die, and ask to be taken out of my body, because I felt so much pain. I saw the rich getting richer and the poor getting poorer. Truly it must be the Mother who wanted me to stay here on the planet, because without a will of my own, it was totally up to the Divine to make sure that I passed through the experiences that I needed to gain my Self Mastery.

In the Self Realized state One comes to understand that there is no experience that has not been self created on some level, that every thing that has occurred has been a balancing of Karma. I have been aware as pain was being released from my body, of some incarnations in which I have been responsible for causing pain in other beings' bodies; such as withholding food from them, taking away their loved ones, and allowing people under me to be whipped.

Whilst staying in this home a Yogi[5] came and said he had been sent by the Eternal Master to assist me and that he would like to

[5] Yogi - from a Sanskrit word 'Yog', which means Yoke or to join up. A Yogi is a person who is stabilized and actively committed to Self Realization.

return with me to New Zealand. He displayed siddhis[6] that hypnotized me in a subtle way, including siddhis to change the weather
and manifest foods and objects.

We decided we would leave together and that I would help
him get a visa for New Zealand. Before we left the village together,
a family I had gone to visit for the afternoon decided they needed
to protect me from this Yogi who could be termed in American
Indian culture a dark force Shaman. This family shut me in a room
while they argued in Punjabi language with this yogi/shaman and
tried to force him to leave me and the village. He left and they were
relieved for me, but then a fierce hailstorm erupted. This was the
dry season when it very rarely rains. The winds came up and a man
came from the yogi/shaman and said that unless they brought me to
a certain house in the village some one would suffer. No one was
able to break the powerful spell being put over me and I wanted to
be with this yogi/shaman. So I was taken on the back of a bicycle
to him. Upon entering his room the storm instantly stopped and I
was unsuspectingly under his power.

My karmas (incompletions) at that time were obviously still
involved with understanding what power was. I was still impressed
on a subtle level by this type of psychic power and was therefore
drawn back again into this type of arena for further lessons. You,
dear reader, would probably be amazed and horrified to clearly see
just how many beings are operating in these levels, and how much
of your own life is affected from this stance of separation. Every
thought which does not acknowledge the ONENESS of the I AM
Presence, which you are as GOD IN ACTION - the truth of this
being the greatest power, is a thought which minimizes your true
GODLY birthright.

In the grip of these karmas we went to New Zealand and
I stayed with him for nine months receiving valuable teachings

---

[6] Siddhis - siddhis can occur on all levels of consciousness. Commonly thought of as an
ability to manipulate the laws of Nature for some extraordinary display of power. These
are phenomenal displays. They in fact do not impact the Oneness and require very little
spiritual development. The siddhis that are of the Oneness arise naturally for the highest
good and cannot be owned by any person.

accompanied by much suffering. At this time I also went through a court case in an attempt to get my son back. My brother had temporary custody of him, and wanted full legal custody. This he achieved.

Feeling the pain at the loss of my son I still understood that somewhere Divine justice was being played out. I felt deep pain at being unjustly judged as a mother - but later came to realize the best thing had happened for Sunjaya, and I was given time alone to rise out of this yogi/shaman's hold over me, and these karmas.

My relationships with my mother and brother were at an all time low. Having them stand in court against me was very painful and I could not speak to them. My nervous system was badly depleted and I started to develop a stutter in my speech. My sister-in-law stood in court and lied about my behavior as a mother, and I was betrayed.

The judge was totally biased in his opinions and religious views, and lived in the same upper middle class suburb as my brother and shared many of the same beliefs.

He labelled me as an unfit mother and wrote in his summoning up that my son was intelligent and should not be subjected to an "Indian lifestyle." With overwhelming odds against me I was forced to give up my beloved Sunjaya.

Mr. Singh (the shaman) was able to enforce his hold over me, as I was weak and vulnerable. My mother lived only a few hundred yards away from us - and we would not see each other. She totally distrusted Mr. Singh - which is a credit to her own pronounced insight. Although she tried to tell me, I had so much anger towards her at this time, I totally ignored every piece of advice she offered.

My son was protected from the energy of this manipulative yogi in a dramatic way by being given over into my brother's caring hands. This time in my life I call my crucifixion.

I eventually found this yogi to be a liar and a thief. He was removing valuables and money from people's homes by the aid of a spirit that he would call upon. This type of spirit form is what I have come to understand as a forth dimensional entity invisible to third dimensional physical eye, yet capable of manipulating or moving form around on a third dimensional level. This forth dimensional activity is not the pure Christ consciousness and is what can be termed as astral karmas when manipulating the field of another soul.

I confronted Mr. Singh when I found much money and some jewelry hidden under his mattress. I told him I realized that he was a thief and that I was going to leave, at which point he became angry and attempted to strangle me. A force picked him up and threw him back about ten feet into the wall. When I asked him what happened he said that his spirit had told him it was not a wise thing to kill me. I was grateful for the intervention of Divine Will, and could only feel compassion for this misguided soul.

As I lay in my bed that night a very brilliant golden light (The Master Koothumi) filled me and the voice said "now is the time to move." I once again understood I had passed through a necessary experience and was freed from the karmas with this soul. I have always had an intrinsic understanding of the perfection in providence[7], and I had come to know that this interaction was a spiritual debt that I needed to free myself from, and that Divine Will was always in command. I needed also to totally understand that the display of miraculous siddhis was no sign of true spiritual enlightenment. There was still within me at that time the naivety to be impressed by siddhis and I needed to have this strong lesson.

The next morning as I walked out from the house I felt a very physical force pulling out from the back of my head and I stepped out of the hypnotic state that I had been under for nine months. It was very tangible and it has allowed me ever since to see this energy in other beings and be able to hold myself above it.

Freeing myself from this energy and Mr. Singh enabled me to have the necessary healing with my mother. I went to live with her - and a few weeks later my brother returned my son to me. This reunion was healing for all of us. I continued a daily two hour Sadhana accepting all conditions. Six months later the mystery

[7] Providence - unavoidable destiny.

again played out its wild card, and in circumstances beyond my control, my son who was now six years of age, was removed again from me by my brother. They wanted him back. In that experience I was thrown into the emptiness in a profound way. I knew how the Buddha felt when He left His family and kingdom. This emptiness is void of all emotion, and all effort to continue to exist ceases. Yet it is not a death wish, it is in fact total acceptance of the transitory nature of all form, and brings an uncanny peace that comes from accepting this reality.

Recently my Beloved and I were invited to stay a few days with a spiritual community, and I came face to face with a male spiritual teacher manifesting the same energy as Mr. Singh - the shaman I had been hypnotized by. He even physically looked a lot like Mr. Singh. It was obvious that the people around were seeking from a disempowered viewpoint, which He consistently reinforced. I talked in length to a few of these people, and saw how the teacher was reinforcing their inherent feelings of lack of Self worth, guilt etc. He had told one lady that she was one of the darkest forces on the planet. This type of subtle manipulation is going on too much, in many so-called spiritual arenas.

Whilst in meditation at this community, the Eternal Master from whom I receive guidance came and clearly showed me the teacher's tendencies, and informed me he was being closely watched (by a group of Masters). I was also asked if I wanted to do anything else about this situation. I realized that I had a choice to act more consciously in total honesty, or remain quiet. I know that this energy does not want to be called out, and that it persists because there are not enough conscious beings on the planet. I took this to be an opportunity for my growth, and let this energy know that it was seen.

The next morning I talked with the teacher and clearly stated lovingly that he had limitations that were not being addressed, and that his spiritual growth involved surrendering to the Mother, and receiving the Grace that would come. To do this he must acknowledge the equality of women, including his own wife, who was obviously under his thumb.

He listened, but did not really hear. His psychic ties into the earth, which he used to draw upon and create a manipulative atmosphere, were subtly cut by the energy of the Goddess. We moved on, and for a couple of days were aware of the psychic kick back. I was happy, because I knew we had made an impact, and that I was a lot stronger.

Chapter Four

INITIATIONS INTO KRIYA YOGA

*Fo*ur months after Sunjaya had returned to my brother, a newly found friend informed me that we were to go to India together. Once again I was on a journey to the Himalayas.

India has always fascinated and repelled me simultaneously. It is a country of total paradox, a country of extremes, and the people are often soft and surrendered, yet can also be gullible and overly emotional. Overall, India appears in a state of decline, with its problems on a vast scale.

Even in this outer state the atmosphere of Divine enlightenment exists in many empowered areas left in the rocks, trees, and air by the awakened yogis and ascended Masters who have graced that continent for thousands of years. I believe this Grace can transform any heart-centered person who meditates in these places.

On our travels we met some devotees of a teacher who claimed to be the Eternal Master BabaJi, though my intuition understood that this person was a fake.

Whilst pregnant, I had read of the existence of the Eternal Master and had a deep knowingness that He was my Eternal Guru and was the unseen force directing all the events in my life. This was very soon to be confirmed, though I did not know it at that time.

As we walked into the valley where this yogi was living with about 100 devotees, mainly of western origin, I was aware of him vibrationally checking me out and could hear him telepathically. We were made welcome and I noticed most of the women had shaved their heads. This felt to me like a cutting off of their own strength, and I have since come to totally realize that the hair is in fact our etheric grounding into the body and a very important stabilizer of the Kundalini strength in the physical body. One way to take another's power, is in fact to cut their hair. Something this teacher was exploiting.

In our present culture this is a direct reflection of the state of mass consciousness, and most men are choosing to be subjected to this denial of Higher Self expression in the world of form. Women lose much of their feminine intuitive powers and balance from cutting the hair, and I am very aware of this in my interactions with them.

In this Ashram at Harikahn, I was given the cave of honor to sleep in the first night, as it had been the yogi's cave for his Sadhana. During the night I was conscious of him attempting to gain control over my energy. This intrusion is a form of black magic, fortunately I recognized it immediately.

Having by this stage grown beyond the grip of such beings, I had decided by morning it was time to leave and after being asked to do a certain duty I said no, and that this yogi was in no way my Guru and that I was leaving. This yogi known as "Harikhan Baba" has since that time died, proving that he was not the Eternal Master, yet still many naively continue to worship him. The genuine Eternal Master has a physical immortal body which he created around two-thousand years ago. For Him there is no death and no need to change bodies.

A few days later we were eleven-thousand feet up in the Himalayas, and it was here I met a yogi who had a deep peaceful presence, and we were invited to stay with him. Some of my first words to him were that I was not looking for a Guru; that I did not believe in scriptures or words, that I only believed in my own direct

experience, for that was the only thing I could take with me. He graciously smiled and said that this was the true way, and that I was now ready for further growth.

As I travelled up the mountain to his hut, I remembered seeing this hut four years earlier in a vision. I had also heard certain tones and saw this yogi sitting outside his hut. Yet again the truth of undeniable providence was apparent.

My friend did not feel the same attraction to this yogi and tried to influence me to leave. It became obvious he was unable to accept my new relationship though we had not made any commitment to be as a couple. My friend decided to leave me on the mountain and went his own way, taking our shared savings and leaving me with almost no money. I knew I was spiritually blessed and chose to remain.

This yogi instructed me in various techniques of meditation. It has been a great blessing for me to receive these meditative practices, and three hours daily for six years I applied these in my Sadhana. They assisted me in dissolving the breath and mind and reaching a state of perfect internal equilibrium in which all seeking stopped in that union of Oneness.

This inner peace is bliss itself. As it is deepened, One drinks from the internal nectar. This internal nectar is one of the great secrets of rejuvenation.

It is inappropriate to reveal this Yogi's identity. He had been celibate all his life and had been told by the Eternal Guru that I would come and instruct him in Tantra and that he would be wise to accept this as part of his unavoidable destiny. The Eternal Master said he would be moved out of India to complete karmas from previous incarnations.

It was very difficult for him to enter into intimate relationship with a woman and though we had a deep connection which he enjoyed, he struggled with many past tendencies and images of how he should be, due to his institutionalized conditioning. He had never been with a woman before, as he had lived with his spiritual teacher from a very young age in monastic life. He already had a strong image of how he was expected to be as a Guru, as many people had an established connection with him in this role. He knew they would not accept the fact that he had entered into relation with a woman, as they honored his celibacy. Probably this is why he called me Kali, the name of the Goddess who destroys all illusion.

The practice of Yogic techniques is absolutely essential to transcend limited awareness, yet if one uses these techniques, and denies the fullness of life, these very techniques designed to be liberating become a bondage. Thus they become a means of escape into contraction. In this contracted approach, true happiness, freedom, and a radiant relationship with the Earth's forms are ever elusive.

To totally transcend Maya we must embrace it, die into it, and find our existence beyond form. This is Tantra. Yet it takes a mature soul to know all the subtle intricacies and games of the ego (mind). During the time I was with this yogi it never really occurred to me that I was in fact his teacher, for me I was just being mySelf.

The Goddess has a way of teaching without needing to declare herSelf as a teacher. She is liberated from the attachment to image, being the space in which everything manifests. The Goddess in this sense has the power to transform all men, by dissolving all their attachment to image and form.

In Tantra, especially Red Tantra (sexual union), every limitation just comes up in a natural way through Love, to be examined, recognized, and hopefully released.

All resistance comes up in Love's annihilating embrace, and if we deny our true emotional needs, we will demonstrate various neurotic (self destructive) patterns, and eventually create disease. There is the strong male tendencies to attempt to override the emotional body, by asserting the mental body. This male part of our psyche has to eventually surrender to the feminine and acknowledge EMOTION - Energy in Motion. Before this integration occurs fully beings will continue to manifest struggle and illusion to some degree.

A balanced enlightened human being is for me one who radiates health, inner stillness, and true happiness. I have always measured my progress by the strength of these qualities. By totally observing and working with the energy flows in the body temple, I have gained my greatest insights. The activating flow of the Kundalini opens all the spaces in the body to joy, freedom, and the all seeing omnipotent light. Words are unable to describe the fullness of such experience.

When we acknowledge life as Divine we can participate consciously as God/Goddess in daily relationship, flowing rather than controlling. It is essential to purify the body and the mind, to know the Self beyond the breath, beyond neediness, beyond separation, then relationship can be a healthy fulfillment of the Divine Will.

This knowing of Self beyond separation takes years of Self inquiry and disciplines which are introspective. It will not happen as long as one is using something external as their security. Once established in the Self, the Divine Will automatically does what is the "highest good" for us, and we can free people and things from our possessive neediness. This allows karmas to be completed speedily, so we may move steadily forwards in our goal towards true freedom and happiness. Fortunately I realized by the time my son was three years old that he was not "mine" - He is a soul-mate very dear to me, with his individual destiny and necessity to gain his own experience. The pain I felt at our separation was part of my own resistance to Divine Will. It takes time for us to be broken down egoically. It takes time for the Supreme power to bring us back home into alignment with the "DIVINE ONENESS." We need to be patient with ourselves and others in this unparalleled process. I gained much needed patience and forebearance through the application of these newly transmitted Kriya[1] techniques.

---

[1] Kriya - Meditative techniques to create a still and vibrant inner focus in which to develop a deep relationship with the Soul, and to receive the Grace of further openings.

The Swami I was now involved with, including sexually, was undergoing major re-alignment. Remember he had been celibate for all his life - over forty years, and he had been brought up in a monastic environment.

Many spiritual teachers have felt impelled to be secretive on the very subject of their sexual activities, and often necessary understanding has consistently been put behind closed doors. It is no wonder that there is so much confusion in the arena of sexuality on this earth.

Those teachers who behave hypocritically know in their hearts that this is not tolerated by the Mother and they will have to return, to grow into greater conscious expression.

After being together a couple of months the Yogi had to travel to continue his teachings to his devotees. I followed him some two weeks later. We stayed in the home of his long time devotees. He had become reserved and would not express affection for me in others' company. I was expected to conform to the image his other devotees had of him. This I would not do - and started yelling at him that I could not have anything to do with hypocrisy. I caused a scene which no-one wanted and I am sure the family was happy to see me leave. The Yogi and I agreed we would be apart until he left India. He said our relationship could flourish in USA where he could be more free. He suggested I go to Australia and see my son.

In Australia I once again had contact with Sunjaya, now aged seven, and within a few weeks he made the decision himself that he wished to live with me. He has always been a great joy in my life.

My brother did not try to stop my son, though it was painful for him to let Sunjaya go.

The Mother as always blessed us with a beautiful peace-filled environment and luxurious home to live in with affordable rent. We enjoyed motoring in our little row boat to and from the island our home was situated on. This beautiful area in Sydney is called Church Point.

It has become my regular experience that all events were and are always perfectly orchestrated by the Oneness, and all we need do is surrender to our own co-created perfection in this wonderful leela[2]. By surrendering we no longer need to experience struggle, fear, doubt, or lack of anything. We always have exactly what we need, every moment. This is a great truth. I have never needed to own things of the earth. They come and they go in the momentum of my providence. This awareness of non-ownership has given me freedom to be moved easily by the universe (one-mind), and to share more easily.

After one year Sunjaya and I returned to New Zealand and found another perfect place where he could go to a small country school that I liked.

Four months later the Yogi called me to the USA to see if we could establish a life together with my son. Sunjaya was about to have two weeks of school holiday and my father and his new wife came to stay with him in our lovely home on the ocean. It was not easy for me to leave Sunjaya for these weeks - but the yogi had written and said that he would **die,** if I did not come.

I went for three weeks, totally open to the possible. We found we could not accept each other's differences. He felt I was too willful, and not subservient enough to him. I remember saying to him that it was very difficult, as I had been brought up in a western independent environment, and I needed equality within any rela-tionship, and the restrictions on me were stifling. I also saw he would have great difficulty adjusting to responsible selfless parenting.

---

[2] Leela - Divinely orchestrated dance of change

His body was experiencing a lot of pain from the changes in his environment. A dense Californian city is very different from living in the pure rarefied atmosphere of the Himalayas. I massaged him daily and wanted to get him outside to physically exercise. He was very used to dissolving in meditation for many hours on end, and had no interest in physical activities. I respected greatly the spiritual achievements and dedication of this teacher - yet I also saw the areas of growth still necessary for him to become happy and liberated.

To be able to integrate change, one must be willing to bring in new concepts and expand and flow rather than resist. His pain at this time was due to his unwillingness to acknowledge his underlying emotions, and to express them so the energy could move and change. He was blocking himself. I felt there was not enough self-honesty and did not want to stay with this contraction and unaddressed unhappiness around me. Even though I loved him greatly, I had to honor my truth and leave, after being with him three weeks.

I had also promised Sunjaya I would be away no longer than three weeks, and happily returned to him.

This Yogi continues to live alone, quietly gathering a following of disciples in California. He writes books and has bought himself a home.

Chapter Five

CONVENTIONAL LIFE

*T*he next four years were spent in a rural area of New Zealand deepening my practices and maintaining family life. I cultivated gardens, played with Sunjaya, enjoyed him growing, completed a home study course in herbal medicine, grew herbs and administered them to locals along with the healing art of massage, counselling, and Hatha yoga.

I had long since realized that very few people want to make the necessary sacrifices and changes to gain Self Realization. New Zealand is a place where comfortable mediocrity has lulled people into a state of complacent inertia. Here, as elsewhere, most people put the majority of their God Given time and energy into creating a secure, comfortable life for themselves - this all being material and outside of "their inner self." This acquiring of "possessions" includes the idea of owning the car, the house, the wife/husband, children, money. In truth that which we "think" we possess - actually possesses us! In this "idea" one's security is outside of oneself, and leads to **fear** of loss and change. This in turn leads to imprisonment within this framework that people identify with as "their life - their happiness." Dear reader, what do **you** identify with as your source of strength? Be Honest.

My life has had long periods when I have had no-one to share Satsang (Divine association) with, so my inner resourcefulness has needed to be at all times strong to maintain a daily meditative practice. In fact these times with applied practices, have always given me great strength and nourishment, and I have experienced the value of being a silent Yogini, communing with My own inner "Light."

Staying close to nature during these times has strengthened and reflected my inner tranquillity. I suspected that during this time there was more for me, and trusted that at the right time the mystery would unfold another leela (Divine play) for my expansion and enjoyment.

After being with Sunjaya for two years, I married, and I confess that I did at this time compromise my inner truth, by wanting to do "the right thing" in Sunjaya's eyes. Sunjaya desperately wanted a father, and responding to his need, I accepted a proposal of marriage from a man who had privately held the "idea" of marrying me for nine years. Just before the wedding I had my long hair cut very short as a symbolic gesture, knowing I was giving up my power, for this duration.

I cared genuinely for the man I married, but in my heart I knew he was not the one for me. On our honeymoon in Europe whilst visiting his family, the limitations in the marriage were already evident. We were arguing about little things - he wanted to do things I did not, like drinking coffee in sidewalk cafes. One day we were walking in the hills and went up to the top of a waterfall. As we stood on the top quietly, I had a clear recall of being with him in a life in Europe. He had been a severe wealthy land owner, and I was a peasant girl. We were drawn into a passionate relationship, yet I would not bend to his ways. One day when we were out together he had pushed me over that waterfall. Here we were now and I relived all those feelings. After fifteen minutes of silence we turned and walked away. He broke the silence, saying how he had felt feelings to push me over the waterfall. I said " that is because you have done it in the past." I understood clearly now that this relationship was to be another "karmic" completion.

I was feeling pulled to India to meditate and he was pulled to the mountains for hiking. So during our honeymoon we already went our separate ways. This must have seemed strange to his family though they were very polite at all times.

In India I travelled to be near the Ashram where Sri Yukteswar of the Yoga lineage I was now a part of held his Maha Samadhi. This "Maha Samadhi" is the final letting go of the body through a total conscious exiting at the time called death. Death of course is a no thing. I wonder why we do not acknowledge it as "transition" instead. Here I stayed a couple of weeks before returning to Sunjaya and married life. I played my part and did my best. The man I married was happy as he had entertained ideas of marrying me for almost ten years.

We lived very simply and Sunjaya was happy. I had no high expectations of our marriage and very soon there was a distant unspoken air about the relationship. We had virtually no intimacy and slept in separate beds. I escaped into my meditations. During this time I maintained my inner Love affair with the unseen Eternal Beloved. Through this inner communion I felt Loved, nourished, and fulfilled. Upon meeting my Beloved in 1987 I realized it was He that I had been reaching out to at this time and was connecting with him on the Etheric planes. This is the natural function of the Twin Ray, that the male and female guide and encourage one another until they are "ripe" for their completion together into "Christ" consciousness, and full body ascension.

My husband had no interest in spiritual practices at this time, and was devoid of yearning to change anything. I understood that life, *(i.e.* my destiny), would change things at the right time.

Two years into the marriage, I received the inner call to go to California. This felt very uncomfortable as California was the last place on earth I wanted to be, or take Sunjaya to. This is how the mystery always works, and any resistance I have ever had, I have been brought face to face with by Divine Grace. I have always been given the opportunity to overcome my limitations and resistance.

The inner call was reinforced with two events. Firstly my brother wrote requesting that he be able to take Sunjaya to Disneyland on a two week holiday in Los Angeles. Naturally my son said he would like to go. Secondly I received a letter from a friend in California, that I had not had contact with for seven years, inviting me to come. What I wish to convey is how every detail is taken care of when one totally lives in trust and service to the Divine. In this situation, as it has happened for me many times, I personally did not have the finance available for plane tickets and travel. During my Sadhana I was instructed to go and ask a certain couple that

I had counselled, for the finance I needed for this journey. Obeying - with full confidence in Divine Will - I was received with grace, and willingness to help. Also they mentioned I need not feel pressure to pay them back. This amount was little for them - and I was grateful to the Divine.

All was arranged in a very short time, and it was decided that I would go two weeks ahead of Sunjaya's proposed Disneyland holiday, to see if we could make a home there. My marriage was on totally unstable ground and this certainly felt like its completion.

I have always found that when Divine providence is to the fore, things will arrange themselves and opportunities are presented to gracefully bring to fruition what is being asked of one. What is needed is courage and trust. Remaining surrendered and aligned has been my key to Grace-filled events, and seeing the perfection in all situations, has consistently proven life to be meditation itself. Leaving the tranquillity of the bush, trees, river and birds was difficult, as silence with nature has always been a preference for me.

In California I was exposed to different attitudes and denser vibrations. The first week I was in shock and cried as I sat on the Earth and felt all the imbalances created by insensitive beings. I was amazed at the extravagant use of what I see as precious resources.

People seemed to yell a lot at each other in normal conversations and the stress levels were greater than I had ever experienced, the result of getting caught up in materialistic struggles. At the same time I knew I could grow in this experience. I also entered into a strong tantric relationship, which was beneficial to myself and partner. I had strengthened my spiritual practices and stabilized the opening of certain chakras during the five years of Kriya[1] practices. As a Tantric Yogini I understood it was now time to allow the opening of all my chakras in a stronger way. My partner had been practising spiritual disciplines for many lifetimes, and was suitable for this exchange. There was in fact a strong recall of us working together in this way in Egypt.

---

[1] Kriya - technique for purification to harmonize and elevate conscious awareness.

The expected arrival of Sunjaya did not happen. A family member became ill, so the holiday was cancelled, and he chose to go and live with my brother in Australia who represented to him a needed stable environment. He was understandably hurt and angry, as in his eyes I had once again disrupted his family life. Though I called him by phone to say I wanted him with me, it was not to happen and he was released into another experience. It took three years for me to totally release him and get over the pain of feeling a loss, and questioning "did I do the best thing?"

It all comes down to total surrender, owning One's aloneness with God, being totally honest and taking full responsibility, and knowing that one's actions were made for the highest good. Also acknowledging one's own and other's karmas to be completed and the personal destiny to be fulfilled.

It was also made known to me that Sunjaya had chosen me as his mother so that he could be set free at a very early age to experience what he needed to, without my biased, and sometimes overly-protective influence.

He has a specific spiritual purpose for this incarnation and I have no doubts that it will come into his conscious awareness within the near future.

Chapter Six

MAFU AND THE EXTRA-TERRESTRIALS

*I*n California in 1986 I was introduced to a new reality and new way of teaching, which is very fashionable at present. It is called channelling[1]. This particular form was a totally unconscious channel taken over by another soul. The channel in this process went through an experience similar to the death process, and totally exited bodily consciousness, allowing another soul to enter her body.

The enlightened energy of the teacher who came through was very forceful and those of us who were in his presence were introduced to some wonderfully empowering revelations and knowingness. I was sceptical for the first hour or two, then this teacher called Mafu came to me personally and said I was a great being of Love and that he would assist me to realize more of who I was in totality.

I was very established in my Kriya practices and phenomenal powers were no longer of interest to me, yet I was, and always shall be, open to greater and greater experiences of soul. I began what I now call sixth level initiations, where the veils of separation and non-seeing are removed. In this initiation the 'third eye' is totally opened.

---

[1] Channelling - Being a conduit for a certain expression of consciousness or entity still held in the subconscious or unconscious reality of the channel. Channelling is new age mediumship, and denotes some degree of separation between the message and the messenger.

There are too many events to recall during this period of my awakening, so I shall recall what is uppermost in mind. In the light of the present new age world supermarket I feel the need to bring an overall view of discerning wisdom to help people cut through spiritual materialism, which is rampant.

At this time I chose to sleep outside on the earth to receive the balancing and strength from the Mother to help me integrate what was otherwise at times disorienting. I remember feeling "too big to fit inside houses" and needed the vastness of the sky and earth to dissolve into.

One night whilst sleeping the earth under me felt as though it was opening and I sensed the presence of what people call extra-terrestrials. These beings whom I understood as being from the Pleiades had light bodies about seven feet tall with two arms and legs, very long hands and large egg-shaped heads. They felt very blissful. They conveyed to me a feeling of familiarity and informed me they would assist me in the revelations I was having, and with the energy healing work I was doing with others.

From then on they were with me regularly. One day I saw five of them quite clearly as they appeared in the healing room and gave me knowledge concerning my client's underlying issues that were ready to be brought into the light for healing.

One evening a group of about twelve people went with Mafu down to the ocean. He proceeded to bring down a Pleiadean[2] Mothership[3]. Most people did not have direct telepathic contact, but I did. I was called to walk down the beach alone. When I sat down

---

[2] Pleiadean - 'Play-at-ease', coming from the Pleiades star system (also known as the seven sisters). Some qualities of the Pleiadean Beings include a deep commitment to the alignment and harmony -"Planetary Peacemakers." Ambassadors for planetary peace. The Pleiadean Star system compromises mostly forth and fifth dimensional-based civilizations, and contains enlightened members known as the "Golden Pleiadeans." It is these Masters that I have had much contact with on an etheric level. The Pleiades Star systems are very active in shaping the future of this Earth.

[3] Mothership - where the E.T.'s have their parties. A collectively held focus for dimensional and interdimensional travel or relocation. A Mothership denotes a large vehicle for this purpose, sometimes consisting of hundreds or thousands of souls working together.

two of these Pleiadean beings began communicating telepathically with me, I felt their hands on mine but could not see them.

When I asked "Why can I not see you?" They answered that it was better that I hear rather than see them at that moment. I felt they were interrogating the very core of my beingness and they asked what my intentions on the earth were. I said to bring Love, as for me that is the greatest transforming power. They said they would always be with me, and that they could only come close to beings who were beyond fear, for fear often turns to anger and, these vibrations were too harsh for them to be near.

During the next months I experienced molecular changes in my body. My sensitivity to thoughts was much greater, and I felt my brain undergoing what I call "rewiring." I became more conscious at night of leaving my body and going into their spaceships, where I would be laid out with crystals and had lasers of light and sounds integrating my etheric body more consciously into physical alignment.

My whole beingness felt lighter and I began laughing a lot more at everything around me, and took myself less seriously.

They informed me that my healing of others was from then on to be carried out vibrationally and that I should not touch other people's bodies as in massaging. I understood, and it felt right, and it was an indication of my heightened abilities to transmit light to others.

During sleep I was informed on the inner planes by Mafu that I was an inner earth being[4] and that I had never felt at home with most people on this earth.

Mafu then took me on a journey through the inner realms to the place I called home, that can only be described as existing beyond the light, where there is no separation, only the existence of Oneness. Mafu told us he was one of the seven stars of the Pleiades and belonged to what is called the Brotherhood of the Seven. He is a great God Master.

---

[4] Refer to Chapter Eighteen on Inner Earth & Rainbow beings for explanation.

I understood that this is where I had been before coming into incarnation. There is a continuum of consciousness that exists beyond what we term life and death. In truth there is no life or death, and even to use the terminology, "having many lifetimes," is a limited expression of the truth of continuum. We in truth just ARE. We are not born, and do not die. This is a great Realization. When one realigns one's consciousness to this reality, great joy comes. In this awareness we no longer feel the pain of separation, which is apparent death. The words used "to die daily," is a great truth. All this means is that we regularly dissolve our separative conscious awareness into the great flowing Oneness. In this state all struggle ceases.

Each embodiment is a grand opportunity to awaken fully into this eternal reality. We carry with us both the limiting tendencies, and the wisdom gained in each embodiment. As long as we see ourSelf as separate in any way, we will be creating karma or unfinished business, so to speak, to a greater or lesser degree. All this disappears in total Realization, and we witness ourSelf as the same through every apparent experience in time and space. In this realization we know ourselves and all beings as extra-terrestrials (to know oneself beyond terra or earth).

During this time of reactivation I was taken regularly onto the spaceships of these "Golden Beings" for realignment of my etheric and emotional and mental realities. This realignment was performed with the assistance of crystal and laser technology including sound and color. I was aware of my surroundings and our telepathic conversations. It was an ecstatic enlightening time - with beings I felt as my true family of Love and Light. I wanted to be with them in all ways - and welcomed all my activations of seeing hearing and communication clearly on these more refined levels. This interaction with my Extra terrestrial family continued regularly over a period of approximately one year. I needed their loving support and they gave easily.

I was now able to take others into the crystal and laser energy ships for realigning and reawakening the etheric body. I found that people must be spiritually prepared for these experiences, or else they are unable to integrate the realignments into the physical. In this inability to integrate the "highest good" distortions occur, and no real spiritual growth is stabilized.

One evening Mafu told me I had three days to heal the sprained ankle I had incurred whilst hiking. He said I was going to be called. Sure enough, three days later I went into the canyons behind the town unexpectedly with a friend. As we walked in I become aware of being called telepathically to a particular spot and we lay down on the rocks and I assisted her release of emotions through rebirthing[5]. She was being activated by the energy around us. I became aware of a distinct low droning tone and felt a spaceship right over me. It was as though I was sucked up into it and the ship then became the whole earth and I became the earth also. A profound feeling of connectedness was experienced, as I realized "I Was the bliss of creation itself." This lasted maybe forty minutes as I sat in meditation.

---

[5] This is a technique of applying exaggerated breath to open blockages in one's emotional body.

What I came to see during this time in California, is that as one receives the Grace of these awakenings, one must continue to be even more diligent in purification lest spiritual ego takes over. This is what is called the time of "Shaktipat" in a seeker's life when phenomena can entice the aspirant into delusions of special-ness and grandeur. This I have seen happening with others, and have come to see how the aspirants may be caught up for lifetimes with these feelings of special-ness, and use their gained enlightenment to impress others, for name and fame etc. This happens as a result of not maintaining spiritual disciplines, and a lack of humility[6].

My morning five am Sadhana remained throughout this time though I found it changed, as I realized I had matured in my practice of certain Pranayama and Kriyas.

Mafu informed me that I must release all judgement of past experiences and the hurts that had caused these judgements. This is the inner work necessary to stabilize the higher initiations into the body temple.

This was intense, and at times I felt as if knives were penetrating, particularly in my third chakra, as the cellular memory of events were bought up, and passed like a movie on the inner screen. I experienced the total abuse of the feminine power and relived the rage I felt at watching injustices, especially during the time of Lemuria and Atlantis.

I also saw my limitation to love intimately, too freely, without wisdom, and consequently suffering as a result of my naivety and expectations. There remains a great deal of pain and anger in women who have given themselves emotionally and physically without being first enlightened. Now is the time for this healing and transcendence to occur on Earth for the birth of the Goddess. In these situations, I saw how I had often felt trapped in a situation, and could see no better course of action. This was with the hope that the party concerned would change a particular habitual pattern. I saw also how I had allowed myself at times to be a dumping ground

[6] Willingness to constantly look to OneSelf and see what can be improved.

of other's insensitivity because of my lack of discrimination. Also I saw the helplessness of taking incarnation for the upliftment of others - what I call the inevitable ordeal.

The way of spiritual growth is inevitably through powerful tests and lessons here on earth. There is no way out, only through, and we as a humanity are existing simultaneously on many levels together. This means that as One becomes clear or enlightened, One immediately becomes more aware of the painful condition of most people's existence in their unconsciousness. When the state of clarity is Realized, One who chooses to remain in service on the earth is to some degree in a state of sacrifice.

In Indian scriptural literature, the beings who are clear and called enlightened, who serve humanity out of pure Love, are referred to as Boddhisattvas. They serve in the Oneness for the upliftment of humanity. There are many ways to serve in this consciousness, and many choose to serve outside of a religious organization.

All our pain comes from a thought of separateness. Understanding this was a great realization, and the constant realignment into the only true state of Oneness continued. I realigned at this time to knowing that my beingness is multidimensional and that my Pleiadean and Extraterrestrial contact was a re-connection with the consciousness "I Am," existing beyond the limitations of earth's social consciousness. I have recalled my identity with star systems and planets including Pleiades, Venus, and Orion, and have intrinsic understanding of the many other planetary and star learning grounds.

It was from this understanding that I truly began to feel the power of my newly regained freedom. I understood that I exist simultaneously on the earth, within the stars, and within the earth herself. I am therefore undying.

As we recapture this truth and align to the power of the pure white light of identity, it brings certainty and confident expression. This is why we must always remember the first, true spiritual virtue is humility. In this way we can assist others effectively.

The timing for each soul's awakening is ordained by many and varying reasons, and awakening carries with it the ability to be more responsible to other Ones not yet awoken. This timing, or release of Karmas, is overseen always by the ascended Masters of Love, who never interfere with a souls progress, but are always there to give protection, blessings and guidance. As a soul realigns to spiritual growth and listens to their inner directives, they become known as a neophyte. From here it is Divine timing and providence as to when the neophyte will be connected **consciously** to the Eternal Beloved Ascended Masters.

Chapter Seven

PRIESTLY KARMAS

*I*n my journey of self transformation, I regained my inner vision to see how I and many others have participated through many in-carnations in co-creating and perpetuating various different limited realities, which we have agreed to maintain for a certain experience. This insight was accentuated for me whilst in California.

This is all the play or Divine leela which is masterfully orchestrated by the ONENESS through a myriad of diverse ways, which have influenced those of us as we play in certain arenas. All this has been for growth, and as I purified and decided to take more self responsibility for my actions along with acknowledging myself as a totally Divine perfect expression of the Oneness, I have completed karmic interactions and chosen to stop participating in these arenas. I have done this in order to bring into manifestation the "Goddess I Am," and to allow greater experience within the multitudinous potential expressions of the One Self.

One of these arenas of karmic participation is what I have come to term the priesthood and priestess conflict. Certain groups of souls coming onto this planet for the first time, resisted the taking on of a physical body, which is the resistance to being on Earth. One such soul group had a highly developed mental body and felt frustrated by physical limitation. They felt they should be able to manifest whatever they wanted, and they fell into separation and conflict. Not holding on to the "Light of Oneness" which had ordained this experience of Earth (physical embodiment) they resisted the knowledge of the perfection of the "Oneness" and arrogantly disobeyed the ascended Masters of Oneness who were here to guide a myriad of soul expressions to function and blend harmoniously into a great light of Oneness with the Earth. These Masters of Oneness know the earth as a "ONE" collective Light body - of which we humans are all part. As the "Oneness" was denied and distorted by many souls the "One Light" was withdrawn from the surface of the earth into the core or inner ethers of the Earth Body. They were now bound by their actions and would remain so until surrendering to the earth itself, by honoring totally the feminine principle.

These beings, many of whom came in during the Lemurian/Atlantean epoch around sixty-thousand years ago, collectively agreed to create a hierarchy in which they could maintain themselves at the top in a dominating position to receiving the fruits of another soul's labors.

These beings judged the feminine power as inferior, for the feminine expression was the surrender to physical incarnation and took the role of birthing through the body process, rather than through thought, which had been possible in fifth dimensional realms. This physical birthing was painful, because matter itself is contraction of the light of the soul. The male energy judged the female as inferior for expressing pain and the female consciousness bought into that judgement. In buying into this judgement, the feminine energy lost its power of earthly expression and its connectivity to the perfection of the ONENESS, which is the source of all power. This male energy out of balance actually *feared* totally relinquishing all the astral powers to the earth, fearing they would become helpless and disempowered. Some of these beings set about creating structures in which they could hold control. By taking resources, creating barter systems, and monitoring the movements of people, they managed to alter people's beliefs which meant no-one was free.

This is how the priesthood began and throughout history these beings have incarnated time and time again into these structures to maintain control over, and lead those beings who judged themselves as inferior and whom are dependent on an outside power. So began religion, politics, and economic competition.

This of course has never been pleasing to the Mother - An insult to the all encompassing compassion and abundance She Is. Many of these women in Self judgement have been initiated into the cosmic mysteries and held positions as priestesses in the mystery schools throughout various cultures and civilizations. They have understood partial truths and gained limited psychic powers and worked side by side with the priests. These priestesses have known on a soul level the great limitations they were participating in, and have felt the pain of the Mother in the activities of half truths. By still holding the original Self judgement, the feminine power has been weakened and unable to weld the power of the "light" strong enough to overcome suppression and their limited creations on Earth.

Priestly men often use their mental will covertly over the emotional will of women, whilst suffering from fear of absolute surrender to their own inner and outer feminine power and the freedom and Grace which that surrender brings. The priestesses suffer from lack of totally self honest expression and powerful action under their own momentum, and look to men as their security. Whilst unenlightened (unclear) they remain confused which comes through in all relationships.

I bring this into the light with a prayer for reconciliation and healing, so that we may all enjoy true freedom more fully. By releasing all fear we no longer need to hold onto any judgement. Love is absolute freedom. This the Mother knows well and instructs her children accordingly. The priesthood needs the Mother's Grace, these priestly souls will never feel totally at ease on the earth until the ego mind is transcended and all their chakras are opened into the "ONE," and they can then give up the need to dominate others to feel powerful. They will receive Grace by honoring and bowing to the Goddess as She appears!

The priestesses need to reconnect fully to their truthful Self expression, connecting to Earth and beyond into the Central Sun[1] where there is no duality. This is achieved through deep Sadhana, standing in One's own light, and communing with all of existence. They will need no longer to seek approval outside of themselves and will no longer engage in self-defeating relationships or within structures of half truths. Nor will they feel the need to *have to* change others, which is the covert use of the feminine, avoiding looking at One's own self-created difficulties.

The following personal experience is an example of how we can reveal and eliminate karmic cellular memory, and any other unwanted psychic contraction.

During my stay in California whilst undergoing my initiations, I was staying for a few days in the home of some newly-met acquaintances. On my second or third morning I awoke with sharp knife-like pains in my abdominal navel area. Immediately I began breathing in a powerfully exaggerated way so as not to contract into the pain. Whilst breathing in this consciously directed manner, I received some inner pictures. They were familiar as they had come to the surface previously at an earlier time, but had not been completely understood and relinquished.

Intuitively I knew that this issue was coming to the surface for clearing and it was being stimulated by a man in that house who was directly involved in the activation of this. I called to this man to come and be with me during this, but he chose to go out. He had a pattern of avoiding and suppressing any emotional issues. I proceeded to unveil an experience of a previous embodiment in which I was a young woman living on the European moors during medieval times. This young woman was aware of a monk who regularly stood on a hill, watching her below, and feeling magnetically attracted to him she made contact. They became lovers. The monk

---

[1] Central Sun - is the inner point of Oneness as it radiates to all of creation in this galaxy. Thus the Central Sun is an inward opening into Oneness, collapsing all distance and separation into itself. Physically the Central Sun is both the innermost center of any object or person, and also the center of the Galaxy. It is accessible through the inner earth.

invited her into the monastery and requested that she make love with certain other monks, as he was the head monk. The young woman declined as she was only in love with this man. She was then taken into the dungeons and bound to a table. The monk with others, then disemboweled her, cutting her open from her vagina to her navel. The rage that was incurred at that time by that soul, who was me, and every other woman who has undergone this brutality, was still in my cellular memory, and had been restimulated by the reappearance of that monk, who was the man in the house this present lifetime. It was a wonderful healing and revelation, and I saw how that fear was now released and how I was now beyond the grip of this suppressive energy.

When the man who lived in the house returned, he was very upset as he had taken a bad fall from his bicycle. His right hand and arm were very badly bruised and grazed. It became obvious in that moment that as he did not have the courage to face the light, he had incurred payment for this action by falling off his bike. The law is perfect. In this embodiment that man is very psychic, works as an astrologer, is sexually repressed, and has great difficulty entering into intimate relationship.

Since this release I clearly see which men still carry around these tendencies and how they continue to manifest confusion in their emotional sexual experiences. They all have the same tendencies of being unable to surrender, because they need to maintain a position of control.

This priestly Karma rides on the energy of Self-doubting women who open themselves to control and manipulation and attract continuous abuse mentally and emotionally in their lives, whilst often hoping to change the man. Many of these men are outwardly attractive and very skilled in the art of manipulation, what social consciousness calls "charisma."

Please understand these tendencies are mostly carried out subconsciously - that is with only partial awareness of what people are co-creating. When we want to become totally conscious in the One Light, and are willing to look at all the underlying energy of our limitations - we regain the inner vision and power to release all our fear and doubt. Then we can choose how we wish to continue, more consciously participating in our co-creation. First we must want to be fully Christ conscious, awake and happy, then purify and align ourselves into this greater Self expression.

The male must eventually surrender and find his own feminine power within, and the female must eventually expand and find her own male within. This is the coming together of the opposites within each one of us, to become whole and Divinely happy. The process is always, always, always, about Self, and we come to realize that nobody is "out there" doing anything to us, we are creating our reality every moment and having it reinforced by our creations around us. What a joy to be conscious. Free to enjoy ecstatic emptiness and fullness simultaneously. No battles any more to fight. Nothing to gain and nothing to lose.

Chapter Eight

THE GREAT
WHITE
BROTHERHOOD

*Sh*ortly after meeting Mafu I was introduced to another channelled Master. This Master was One of the Ascended Masters of the Great White Brotherhood, which is the name given to the Masters who serve in the Oneness of the White Light for the upliftment of humanity. (Boddhisattvas). The Masters have physically eternal bodies.

I had heard the name The Great White Brotherhood, but had no further conscious understanding of their existence or purpose. It had never occurred to me that I could have a teacher on the inner planes, who would instruct me in as much depth as a teacher of close physical proximity.

My first evening's introduction to this Great Master was attended with approximately seven other people in a private home. The energy of this channelled Master was very refined, like a balm to my soul, and I knew this being in a profound way. The energy was aligned to my natural expression, so it was easy for me to engage in conversation with this Master.

This Master is known as the God of freedom to the earth and all humanity, and as Lord of the Violet ray which is my primary ray of expression in this life. The Violet ray is also known as the seventh ray, and as the expression of refined spiritual eloquence and individual freedom. The deep affinity we shared was because of previous embodiments when we lived in the same family. Saint Germain is that Master's name. He was known as Count Rakoczi in his life in Europe during the 1800's, and has a history of being active in political arenas, not only at that time but also as the first Merlin in England. Some of his other incarnations have been as Christopher Columbus and Joseph the Father of Jesus. In both these embodiments I have been very close to him. As Count Rakoczi he attained the Eternal body and ascended with the name Saint Germain - Lord of the Violet Ray. Attaining the Eternal body he remains physically accessible to advanced adepts on the Earth plane, and he, along with other Beloved Eternal Ascended Masters, will show their presence to more of humanity by the end of this century. This he personally told me in my first private session with him, following the first group evening.

During our first reconnection he had told me to remember my dreams, and this I instantly started doing. Of course this was His blessing upon me. As I sat with him privately I related my dream where I had seen his boat in harbor and was meeting him off the boat. Beside me had stood a young boy and I knew we were family. He responded by saying I had been his sister in law at that time and had cared for his son after the death of his wife. He said we had a great eternal love for each other and that he still wore the clothes I had made him for his journeys as Christopher Columbus. The whole session with him was a profoundly moving interaction - as picture after picture flooded my inner vision of our shared experiences and feelings. This was an instant reconnection to my knowingness of my ongoing service to humanity, along with my growth. He acknowledged me as a great teacher and a teacher to those I had called teachers.

He empowered me into the knowingness of my greater destiny and the words exchanged at that time have helped me tremendously. Saint Germain from that time of **re-cognition** has been a major influencing factor in my life and momentum. For the past six years, Saint German's guidance from the inner planes is always clear, and highly beneficial. He has guided us on pilgrimages, suggested what vortices we should visit, has left clues as to his imminent presence, and has patiently watched us grow stronger. Chastising me when necessary with his most insightful Loving power he has strengthened our Eternal Bond. There is no thing I could ever write or say that could do justice to the Love and Power of Beloved Saint Germain and the other Eternal Masters. The only way we can stand beside them is to awaken to our total Divinity and emulate them in our thoughts, words and deeds. We are in fact in this way working as "the body of the ONE."

Observing other people around the channelling circles of Saint Germain and Mafu I became aware of the limitations in this type of teaching.

I saw that people tend to remain deluded, if they are not applying themselves in a transformative spiritual practice. One does not come up against their ego as is the case under the guidance and presence of a full bodied Master. Spiritual disciplines are usually enforced as being an essential ingredient for Self Realization, the essential preliminary preparation of purification and emptying of "ego-mind." Therefore channelled teachings are for many an escape into yet another fantasy of the ego-mind which loves to hang onto outer power and make psychic phenomena the goal. The varied expressions of channelling represent differing stages of spiritual attainment of the channeller. There are those channels who total-ly exit bodily consciousness and are empty vessels for the higher Self in a Master's form to come through. There are also many who retain mind awareness, yet claim a totally separate entity comes through them. This is often a subtle aspect of their Self connecting to a previous embodiment, or an energy of which they are a radia-tion. It is a great limitation if one stays in separation as a channel. For this reason I have made the clear distinction and do not call myself a channel. A Christed being is totally Self awoken and does not recognize the mind of the "ONE" as separate from "his/her" own. While I now have inner dialogue with many beings, which some would call channelling, I simply look upon it as conscious communications of the "ONE." Remember, we are all channels of some particular frequency and vibratory expression. What is it that you wish to channel dear reader?

My Beloved and I are constantly in inner communion with a number of the White Brotherhood Ascended Masters and they continue to shape and decree our movements, and transmit much of the inner guidance we give others.

THESE GREAT BELOVED ASCENDED MASTERS KNOW THE ENERGY, EVERY THOUGHT, AND ACTION OF ALL SOULS REACHING INTO THE ONE ETERNAL LIGHT. THEY GUIDE AND DIRECT ALL SPIRITUAL ADVANCEMENT ON THIS EARTH, AND WE CAN NEVER CEASE TO PRAISE THE IMMENSITY OF THEIR UNLIMITED LOVE AND GRACE TO HUMANKIND.

The Great White Brotherhood is a vast number of enlightened beings who serve the planetary evolutionary process. The pinnacle of our enlightened state is to become an Eternal Ascended Master. Some of the Eternal Masters have been assigned to the position of planetary lords of the rays of light on which souls descend into physical birth. The Masters names for each ray, are:

Djwal Kul	Master of the Red ray.
Serapis	Master of the Orange ray.
Koothumi	Master of the Gold ray.
Hilarion	Master of the Green ray.
El Morya	Master of the Blue ray.
St. Germain	Master of the Violet ray.

Master of the Pink ray is the Master **Jesus** and **Mother Mary**.

All these beings have had many incarnations on the earth and are all integral parts of a wonderful Divine evolutionary plan for the souls of this Earth.

At times, incarnations have put these souls in world arenas, and at other times they have been unheard of and insignificant. All these beings are conscious of their origin which I call Love. This place of origin has another name, the Central Sun, or land of the Golden Buddhas. It is the space of absolute purity and everyone exists as the One awareness which knows no limitation.

The Brotherhood is at work in many unseen ways, assisting those souls reaching for growth here on Earth. They work with souls from the level of novices, practitioners, and initiates, to adepts.

I recall some of my own experiences with the Masters assisting me through dreams and visions, as an example that anyone on the "Path" of spiritual evolvement will receive all the help they need when the timing is right. One may not even consciously know of the Ascended Masters assistance when this happens, but at some time if the growth continues One will have the veils of separation removed and will be introduced on the inner planes to those Masters, and ones knowledge and joy shall expand vastly.

Their work is profound and absolutely vital to the ongoing evolution for this Earth.

This brotherhood assists us greatly with constant inner guidance, as a result of committing our beingness into service with them. This I call awakened Love. By becoming consciously conscious, one automatically impacts those who are willing to wake up, and through service one is given responsibility for how to be of most value. The Ascended Masters and the Brotherhood serve the unfoldment of the Divine Plan on earth, and see that this unfoldment happens as gracefully as possible for mankind.

There is no religion in the Brotherhood as all these Masters have transcended the need to be contained within a dogma. Having graduated from the varying schools of thought and practices to the Oneness, the Masters then serve interplanetarily. In this expanded capacity to serve they carry titles such as Chohan, Maha Chohan,

Divine Directors, Maitreya. They are also able to transmit the Light of the One mind through a number of people who are in service to the Light. Therefore the Masters are not ever exclusive to one "channel."

With consistency, I have chosen to move into new experiences and remain transcendent of any dogma or religion, so that I may exemplify the Beloved Ascended master's ideals of the truth of Oneness and Love.

This again is the way of the Goddess, the way of Love and all seeing which is the power of unity and freedom.

Reconnecting with the Ascended Masters has assisted me in realizing my Divine purpose, and I encourage all souls to embrace the existence of the Great White Brotherhood, and to ask guidance from the Ascended Masters of the rays as it is timely, and to obey the guidance. In this way one activates Ones own "I AM" presence and is on the way to Self Mastery. This guidance comes from within, and the karmas incurred by seeking outside of Oneself are completed.

These Masters of "Oneness," ascended in body and mind, emulate the highest possible expression of realization for mankind.

Once a soul has been touched by this "Love" consciousness, they will never be able to rest at peace until they have raised their own frequency to be able to commune constantly side by side with these radiant "ONES." This is the coming home to ones own "I AM" Mastery and presence.

The communion with these Masters is all the inspiration my Beloved and I need to fulfil our commitment to serve the light of an evolving humanity, and expand unceasingly in this "Love and Light."

This 'Love Oneness' is the force which will bring a new order onto the earth. It is bringing a whole new social/political/religious structure, and it is that which each soul needs to align to in order to experience wholeness, peace, abundance, and eternal beingness.

No-one lives outside this great omnipotent, omnipresent Law of 'ONENESS' and right **now** on earth this law is bringing the collective Christing, the birth of the Khalsa, Armageddon, into fruition.

Chapter Nine

CRYSTALS AND CLEARING KARMIC CELLULAR MEMORY

*E*ntering the world of crystals is a stimulating and growth filled experience for almost all beings. Crystals were immediately for me a joyous deeper connection to the inner mysteries.

This reconnection with crystals also occurred during my reactivations and initiations in Santa Barbara, California.

I was given a few crystals, as almost every home I went into had crystals. Spontaneously I began meditating with them - learning the secrets they contained - by holding them and becoming ONE with them. The crystals added to the power of my reactivation.

It felt natural for me to communicate with the crystalline consciousness from the start, and I immediately began integrating them into another form of teaching for me.

I recalled using them in different times, specifically Lumeria, Atlantis, Egypt, and Greece. During these recalls I saw how our use of crystals then was much more advanced and refined than it is today. We were able to consciously influence the weather and the growing of food, maintain pleasant temperatures, heal and communicate telepathically over large areas. I understood the esoteric[1] mysteries they were revealing.

[1] Esoteric - Teachings of the inner mysteries. Esoteric knowledge is contained within certain secretive teachings. As the veils of separation are removed in consciousness, this knowledge comes via the Oneness.

The world of crystals presents to us as humanity a vast potential of realignment and reawakening of our Godliness. They also show us how limited we are currently in our communion with our inner power and power of the Mother Earth as a living body. Having clear recall on my very deep ongoing relationship with the formation of the crystalline matrix of this planet shows me how deeply committed I am to the evolutionary potential of earth. I have held positions of responsibility on earth that impacted many thousands of people. By consciously using the crystal energy and having access to MASTER crystals, I had telepathic resonance which connected me directly to the mass frequency. What I felt, they felt and vice versa: what I sent out, was received. My responsibility was then, as it is now, to the Divine Eternal One "I AM" Presence.

I could monitor the levels of harmony in the people, by using the crystal energy as my intermediary. People at those times of heightened awareness of the planet lived in full obedience to the light and Divine directive. The rulers were Masters of the Oneness and beings of great Light. I also recalled the times when most had lost that obedience to the Oneness and the struggle to gain personal power was paramount. I recalled my pain knowing I could not hold the harmony for the collective consciousness. I was at that time trying to bring awareness of the imminent destruction that the rulers of personal power were bringing forth. They would not listen, and I withdrew my Light and presence from most beings.

The crystals are enlightened rocks. They are the etheric storehouse of the memories contained within our earth. They contain our records as participants on the earth. In this understanding I say it is "The Mother who remembers everything - and our eventual liberation is achieved only through HER GRACE."

If you wish to start etherically reactivating yourself: obtain crystals. Hold them, lie on the earth and meditate with them. Talk to them and listen. They are wonderful aides and guides to your etheric reactivation. The crystals revealed for me many mysteries pertaining to creation of form.

Re-establishing contact with my Pleiadean essence and family has helped to make my understanding of crystal power clearer. I have come to understand the enlightened Pleiadean influence on earth as having Divine authority and capacity to assist in the activating of the molecular etheric awareness of those souls on earth awakening spiritually. The Pleiadean's etheric technology is greatly assisting the small percentage of awakening humankind into "its" Collective Christ Body. The Pleiadean star system contains knowledge that is part of the earth's future. This can also be said of other star energies of a peaceful joyous nature that exist on the forth and fifth dimension. When as humankind we awaken to our "star origins," we draw into our conscious awareness the more refined aspects and Divine qualities which reflect through an awakened soul. Through this awakening we will then collectively come together as enlightened representatives of many star systems melding into the "ONENESS" here on earth. The Pleiadean beings consciously awakening into the "Oneness" on the earth plane at this time will naturally fit into the role of planetary diplomats - communicators of Light - and other roles needing people who can peacefully and consciously align a diversity of energies. My experiences have shown me that the fundamental enlightened Pleiadean quality is growth through alignment. The Pleiadean energy does not move forwards until alignment is obvious. This has created a deeply sensitive and harmonious collective process - with less emphasis on individual assertion. Individual assertiveness is more noticeable in beings who have embodied in star systems such as Orion, Sirius, Antares, and planets such as Uranus. This assertive quality is noticeable on earth in these people.

During my learning with the Pleiadeans I allowed the process of transmutation to occur within my cellular matrix, releasing karmic cellular memory. Being willing to see all my limitations through the Grace of the Mother, I became a more refined instrument to perceive the etheric fabric of existence. The crystals amplified and stimulated this process.

The crystals hold the etheric storehouse of memories of our individual and collective actions and they exist in a frequency that a person can tune into for information pertaining to the creation of matter.

This may sound remarkable, and truly it is. It is so simple and so profound at the same time. I am not a highly educated person, and have little scientific understanding, yet the crystals for me contain unlimited possibilities of discovering the secrets of the universe. I believe we are presently just tapping into the potential conscious use of crystals. Having seen past images of how we used crystal energy to generate all our power needs such as lighting, heat, movement of wind current, control of weather patterns, and rapid growing of food, made me aware of how much more conscious our earth is, than she is given credit for. Harnessing the etheric strength of our earth via the crystal energy, we will as an enlightened humankind demonstrate this energy source again, under the guidance of the Ascended Masters. Crystals respond to thought, they are psycho-active tools, and therefore it is unwise for a spiritually unevolved culture to be given these tools. This knowledge will be released to mankind when we as a group consciousness have declared our unity with the Mother, and will no longer support the manufacture of pollutive self-destructive weapons and technologies.

There are many teachings and vast knowledge to be gained from the crystal energy, for this is the etheric subtle layer of creation, waiting to be awoken in ourselves.

As we heal our past and accept ourselves as peace-filled unlimited consciousness, and release the lower emotional/mental blocks of limited human thought, we are then able to explore our greater Self. Then we must maintain the purity as required to hold this knowledge, and use it wisely as needed. I have come to realize that knowledge has been given to me to become free, and to assist others to awaken. In this arena I find no place for Personal self glorification or a feeling of exclusive superiority. Personal glorification automatically cuts off the Grace of the Oneness and the Mother. Though these beings may become a big fish in a small pond, they never experience the beauty of endless growth.

Crystals are a tool to gain knowledge, and can increase ones psychic influence. People who use knowledge as power over others are frequently attracted to the power of crystals. My Beloved and I have met a number of people who misuse the gift of crystals in this way. These people often horde crystals as though they are trophies. This misuse is demonstrated by those caught in the money, name and fame drama. There is, of course, the understanding that these souls are gaining some needed experience out of all this. It will be a far better planet when this abuse of power no longer needs to be demonstrated.

It is great to have the crystal energy around you if you are committed to spiritual growth. If you are not committed to growth, crystals have a way of bringing to the surface any area which is not being addressed consciously, and turmoil may arise. It is an energy to be respected and I would like to emphasize that. We have been involved in working with the crystal energy to assist us in our spiritual teachings these past six years, and have seen at times what can happen when unready, unprepared people start playing with the power of crystals.

A spiritual practice can be enhanced with crystals by a sincere practitioner who truly wants to wake up on every level, and that for me is the only reason to be involved with crystals. The crystals assist us to awaken our full Divine potential. By connecting to them inwardly, we can repair our etheric connections, and the damaged web of crystalline purity, so becoming more conscious of the inner Light and our Oneness.

Placing crystals on the body for etheric healing can help one make this reconnection. My last words about crystals are: they are great tools, yet by no means are they any substitute for spiritual disciplines. One will need to do more than attend crystal workshops or surround oneSelf with lots of crystals, to become enlightened.

Enjoy!

Chapter Ten

MORE ON SOULMATES AND LETTING GO

My tantric partner in California had completions with other relationships, and it was understood we needed to go in different directions. **Love is allowing all beings to do whatever they need to do for their growth.**

This relationship had been filled with much passion and the intensity of this "activating" time. Though this time was especially expanding for me, my partner was also being "moved." He had attended all the "channelling teachings" with me. His love for me personally had become more important it seemed than his Love of the Divine Will.

He helped me a lot to stay in my body and I am deeply grateful for his Loving strength in this way. I felt he was not meditating deeply enough in the formless realms to be able to remain more as a yogi. By not meditating deeply one becomes too caught up in outer appearances. He began showing signs of jealousy when other men looked at me. I loved him totally and had no thought of other men at this time. I was so blissful and consumed by my inner process. Even the pain of release was blissful as I knew I was growing. It is my belief that he already knew that we were not going to be together for a long time. We never discussed this possibility and enjoyed each other as much as possible. Since leaving him, I have realized he is one of the Osiris beings whom I am deeply connected to. This great soul love means all the Osiris beings are for me what people term soul mates. Relationship with soul mates are always very intense and growthful. Here the longing for Love in a soulmate relationships is demonstrated in many ways and flavors. In these relationships there is a tendency to want to hold on to each other, and often this brings pain. This pain is released in the truth filled realization that only one's Twin Ray is ordained from beyond the personality (personal will) to be eternally bonded with.

It takes great Love to set our nearest and dearest free, when we know we are no longer the best thing for them. Love in that context is letting go of our own fears and apparent needs. I had to set my soulmate free and set myself free to move forward. Knowing the pain he would express if I told him, I decided to leave quietly and wrote him a note instead. We met briefly a few times after I left and he was understanding and loving as always. This separating was very difficult for me, though I did not outwardly admit it. He has now come to accept our separation, knowing I am with my Twin Ray.

During this letting go, I was on a roller coaster and had no idea where it was going to take me. Events were happening very quickly with people around me, and I was in the moment with it all. A great lesson in letting go and trusting my own energy as One with the Divine Will. There was no space for contraction on any level, and I was just saying Yes to the inner flow.

The initiations I had gone through were firstly as a result of doing the "inner work" of spiritual preparation, so that I was able to receive, and secondly being in the presence and teaching of an enlightened energy, *i.e.* the channelled Masters.

Just before leaving Santa Barbara I met another deep soulmate. The Masters were moving me very fast through these karmic completions - by bringing them to my door. This man Paul had also been "opened up and reactivated in his Extraterrestrial or Solar knowingness." He was extremely sensitive and fragile at this time. It was necessary for him and I to spend many hours a day in water - a very graceful way to integrate experiences of an "unearthing" nature. There was "no choice" for either of us. We knew instantly we had to "complete" some past experience.

Around this time I phoned my Kriya teacher and told him of my "extraterrestrial" connections. I guess I was wanting some encouragement as I felt very "out there." He sharply said he had no interest in this reality - and was not wanting to meet those beings. This conversation terminated our outer contact, but not inner providence.

Paul, my newly found soulmate, and I were invited by a friend to fly to Arizona and stay a few days in some healing hot springs. There was an old unused resort near them that we could stay in. Knowing we needed water a lot at this time we gratefully went. This place is a beautiful isolated oasis in the desert. The pools are all naturally created, pure and life giving. We immersed ourselves day and night. During this time we released the karma that had bought us back together.

We had been husband and wife during the timing which felt like Mesopotamia. In these embodiments he was a wealthy trader - and would travel on one of his large sailing vessels for sometimes a year at a time. He always bought me back beautiful gifts and I was surrounded in luxury. Often I feared I would never see him again and began to feel angry that he left me in this way. I also became lonely. On one of his journeys away I took a lover and became pregnant. On the day of his return I went to the outer steps to greet him. My lover unknown to me had hidden himself and when my husband (Paul) was close enough, he attacked him and cut his head off. In the pain of this I took a knife, plunged it into my own abdomen killing the baby and myself. This was a dramatic incomplete finish to our lifetime together. In bringing up this pain of losing each other in this way Paul and I healed many things in ourselves. He realized why he had a deep mistrust of women and why he had felt like he was going around at times without a head. I released my guilt of being unfaithful - and released anger at feeling left behind.

All the sanskaras of these karmas must be released from our cellular memory before we can be truly free. This is another example of my inner work.

Do not judge yourself when these types of memories are activated. Know you are blessed and are freeing yourself from past bindings. Paul and I wanted to spend more time together, yet we knew that there were other callings for both of us. He travelled to Hawaii to complete another relationship.

I left California for New Zealand with strong knowingness of the teaching work that was ahead of me. I had gained so much, and continued to receive more. Californians had passed on the wonderful gift of communication to me. Before this time I was more silent and serious. In California I learned to loosen up, and "get off of it." It was a great learning and now people take me to be American, especially in New Zealand. I really enjoy this ease of expressing myself.

On my return to New Zealand at this time I felt like an extraterrestrial[1], and my bodily sensitivity rejected the density around me. I stayed in my mother's home for a few weeks (she was out of the country). Upon visualizing the type of environment I wanted to be in, I was shown the exact house in meditation (a house I had previously seen along a beach). I found out the owner's name, telephoned, and got the house at the rent I could afford. This home was on a private beach two hours from the city with nearest neighbors one kilometer away.

For the next two and half months I shared meditation and energy opening processes with a few friends on weekends. I was calling out inwardly at this time to be with my Eternal partner, for I knew Eternal relationship was the foundation of Love in form, and that if I was to stay on the planet, it could only be in true Eternal Relationship with my eternal partner. I did not use the word "Beloved" until our meeting, upon which the full understanding of the Beloved was mutually understood.

Paul had arrived from Hawaii - and we spent time together. He had brought a friend Wave and they were both looking for a good time. He demanded absolute freedom yet struggled in his emotions

---

[1] An extra-terrestrial (beyond-earth) is someone who is connected to their self beyond the limitation of merely physical awareness. To know our Self in the stars, inside the Earth, to the know power of thought, to expand into the Central Sun: this is to be an extra-terrestrial.

concerning me. I struggled to hold him in our relationship. It was all very uncomfortable - yet we wanted to hold onto something with each other. One night we were meditating in a circle with a few friends. These friends were refined, sensitive and great to be around. I was feeling happy having others to meditate with. During the meditation I became very aware of El Morya Lord of the Blue Ray walking into the centre of the circle. He stood in

Beloved Ascended Master El Morya

front of me, and in his wonderfully empowered manner told me to "set this soul free!" I got the message...

A few days later we were staying with other friends and Paul and I decided to now go our separate ways. He had a strong ability to put me totally back inside myself and helped me see, that I was feeling a strong pull to go alone to Hawaii. I did not know why. Paul travelled on with Wave and I went into personal retreat and did a three day fast to gain deeper clarity as to my next step.

The inner Masters responded to my call for guidance and informed me that my Eternal partner or Twin Ray was in Hawaii. I intuited we would meet around the Harmonic convergence[2]. During the six months in New Zealand I had attended two new age festivals, and "channelled" quite a lot of information for various people. All this sharing I did spontaneously and freely - not thinking about money. Thinking about my material existence is something that has never been a priority for me. It has always felt uncomfortable when I contracted myself for short periods of time to be focused on the material plane. It is just that I have always felt my unlimitedness

[2] Harmonic Convergence - One of a number of activations and shifts of the Earth's internal energy which results in more full surface manifestation and awareness. This particular occurrence was prophesied for thousands of years and was widely attuned to. It occurred from Aug. 13th- 23rd in 1987, and was centered on Aug. 16-17th.

to some degree. It has been a lesson in humility and patience to see how slow and exacting the way things work on this earth plane. At the time I knew I had to go to Hawaii, I borrowed the airfare from a spiritual sister whom I had helped during one of the festivals. In return I gave her a statue of the Goddess Saraswati, that had been given to me in India by an admirer. I knew the statue was worth more than the airfare and we agreed I would give her the money when I had it.

I went to Maui in June of 1987 not knowing anyone, yet knowing I would be guided. Maui embraced me totally - warm, sensuous, luscious, and green. The Mother is very strong there. The whole island is shaped like the top half of a woman. A perfect soft place to heal the feminine part of one's psyche and one's relationships with oneSelf. I relaxed and played. I immersed myself in the ocean daily and remained alone much of the time. Maui was and still is a place that attracts the "new age" energy. At the time I was there I met quite a few Americans involved in self healing and change. As a Yogini, I was very aware of the varying levels of commitment to pure growth, and observations of most people reinforced my belief that without deep, silent, pure meditation, a soul cannot progress far.

Three weeks before the Harmonic Convergence I met a man whom I shall name Don. He attended a crystal meditation group that I facilitated. Meditating with crystals I found helped many people awaken their inner vision and guidance. Don had come to Maui to get out of the "rat-race" from the U.S. Mainland - and was wanting to heal from an emotionally painful relationship. He was slim, short, intellectual and attractive. He invited me to stay in his home he shared with another man whom I shall call Steven. Don's greatest liability at that time was his ego which was being inflated by the use of a new psychedelic drug called ecstasy. This increased his head fantasies and he was prone to delusions. All this I was about to discover. As a spiritual warrior I knew I was being put in this situation to grow, and to assist where possible. Totally trusting Divine Mother I went to stay in the immaculate, clean, comfortable home. (A change from the beaches where I had been sleeping.) I trusted each step I took would be growthful, empowering and freeing. I instinctively knew I would have to be on guard with this soul at all times. I liked him and Steven, another highly intelligent unstable male. Both these men had a lot to learn about relationships with women. I knew it was a challenge and test for me to stay there.

Steven had a history of intermediate drug abuse which I found out was undoubtedly related to his upbringing. His family was extremely wealthy and were nationally known in political intrigues, and had many problems. His mother had committed suicide by shooting herself - and there was much abuse of money and emotions. Steven lived on inherited money. He had a University Degree from Harvard, in literature. I could see this soul had very advanced training spiritually in past embodiments and was very psychic. His sensitivity always drew him to spiritually seeking - yet he lacked enough self discipline to do purifying elevating practise.

Both these men had great potential spiritually, yet at that time they chose to remain egotistical. I took the ecstasy drug to find out what it did. For me it stimulated my mental body and was great fun. The visionary channel was opened and one could create many "ideas" and reawaken many experiences. It was very easy to see how these men and others could become deluded in the power they thought they wielded. Yes we are all Gods with unlimited ability - yet we are all limited by delusion if that power is for selfish self-contracting achievements. This seeking of individualized power eventually leads to being broken down into true humility. Only in rejoining the ONENESS and surrender to the "Divine Mother" can one ever hold any lasting peace and abundance. With these two men, no matter how clear I wanted to be with them- they never "got it." There was always such murky ground around them. Their own mental and emotional unclarity permeated all their interactions, especially with women.

Women for this type of ego behavior are objects to be possessed or dominated. It is impossible to love this type of man for they do not Love themselves - and always sabotage any loving opportunities. These two men could manipulate themselves into believing all sorts of half truths. It was a new experience of great clarity for me. I knew the "Divine" would move me on at the perfect time. Don had a way of deciding what was best for me, and even told a few people we were going to be married, whilst simultaneously ringing his estranged girlfriend in California telling her he was wanting to renew their relationship. Unknown to me he also told my Beloved Twin Ray this when we all met for the first time. Adding to this mad situation in the house with Don and Steven, Paul and Wave just showed up one day and decided to camp in the downstairs garage. I was enjoying the Divine play - by remaining unattached to day to day events. I have always found in these karmic scenarios its best to remain meditative, and watch the flow. It creates obstruction and difficulty when one tries to control these situations. I knew I would be removed at the "perfect time." This deep trust is the way of the Goddess. In this way the mystery is what is trusted - and through purity and prayer all is taken care of.

On August thirteenth Don and I drove to the far side of Maui to meet a friend of Steven's. Steven felt strongly I needed to meet this person.

August thirteenth was the beginning of the Harmonic Convergence. Astrologically it was the time the Mayans had predicted thousands of years ago that would be the advent of a new golden age of earth. They called this time the end of thirteen hell cycles on earth.

Here in the beauty filled jungle of Kipahulu, Maui, I received the greatest gift that can be granted to a soul. The gift of the Beloved Twin Ray incarnate. Here Don introduced me to my Beloved.

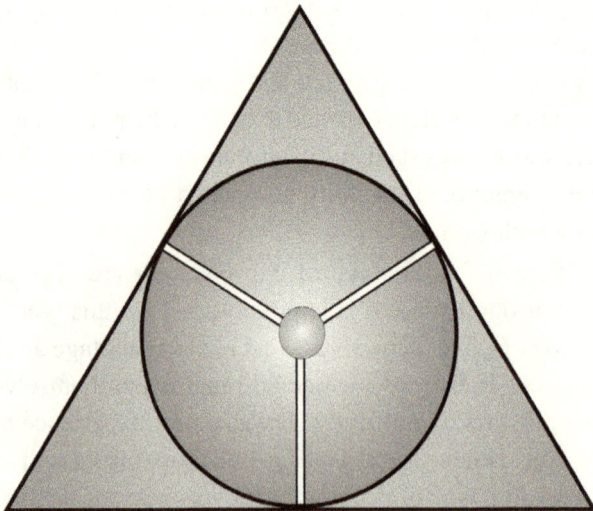

Chapter Eleven

ETERNAL BELOVED RELATIONSHIP

*W*hat is this Eternal Beloved Relationship? There are three forms this relationship takes, and it begins with One's self. When a soul consciously realizes that Love is to be found within and no longer looks for fulfillment through another person, they are beginning the journey towards the "Beloved." This Beloved awakening comes when the soul, after playing in separation, wishes to return to wholeness and Oneness. Through longing, the soul invokes to receive the Grace of an awakened teacher who is called the Sat Guru.

This awakened, freeing relationship brings the first total experience of what in truth Love is. Through this relationship the seeker returning home becomes purified in the fire of Love, and Gracefully the Oneness reveals itself to the disciple (one who is disciplined). The fire of purification ignites the Kundalini and the disciple awakens to his/her own inner light. With this comes the simultaneous realization that the teacher embodies the truths that can be found from within. In this state of Grace we see the light of the teacher and the Light of the student is ONE AND THE SAME.

From this platform we recognize ourself as being equally Divine. This is the ascension in mind. In this awareness, One cultivates the Self as whole and complete, and without need of external relationships to fill the gap of unlovingness within. This is the first understanding of Beloved relationship. It is a level of individual Self mastery earned through surrender and disciplines.

When this merging with one's Divine Self is complete, then the meeting and complete recognition of that perfection in the Twin Flame Relationship can be experienced, if ordained.

The relationship with one's Twin Ray is the outer statement and completion of all karmic relationships in the physical. It is the coming home whilst still in form. There is only one Twin Ray partner for a soul - so there are no choices, for one's twin ray partner is ordained from the first entry into physicality many, many embodiments ago.

This meeting as a Beloved couple is the Christing[1] for those couples who know each other as the Twin Ray in form. This knowledge has all come since meeting my Beloved Twin Ray. Now, one no longer "dreams the dream" of Love incarnate - One awakens the dream and lives it in daily life. In this state the only thing left to "do" is to illumine all of the surrounding creation and to share this frequency with those who also dream of the "Beloved." This is what I now do with my Beloved incarnate.

The third form of the Beloved Relationship is the inner communion with the other conscious Masters of the 'ONENESS." This communion is achieved consciously by dissolving separation forever and going beyond the tenth realm. In the Oneness, one is freed from individual struggle and even the thought that one owns one's body is no longer relevant or necessary. This seeming paradox of giving up all need of power to become all-powerful can only be realized from the level it is attained on.

When my Beloved, Virochana is his present name, and I met there was an instant <u>recognition</u>. We sat down in the grass for a brief few minutes. I was stunned by the depth of purity I saw in this man. It was the most pronounced purity I had seen in One who was also obviously aware of what was going on. I immediately had

---

[1] Christing - Finding the individual Self as a point of expression of the "Oneness" with no resistance and full awareness.

respect for his presence - and
cautiously asked a few days
later if we could spend more
time together. In his lightened
and easy going manner he
answered "of course."

Five days later on
the eighteenth of August, I
took all my belongings out
to stay with him. I arrived at
three in the morning after a
long bumpy truck ride in the
farm truck. Virochana was at
that time working as a laborer
on an organic fruit farm. We instantly experienced the immensely
powerful realization of being betrothed - and our energies being
fused together. From the beginning there were no two beings. It is
the total experience of ONENESS... He is a very advanced Yogi, and
had practised eight years of intense disciplines before meeting me.

We had read no books, had no guidelines, and seen no couples
as twin rays. This subject is of great importance to humanity at this
crucial time, for we believe the Beloved relationship is the beginning
of a new potential dispensation for an enlightened humanity. Hari Ji
(my Beloved's name before changing it to Virochana) had been told
by the Ascended Master Koothumi two weeks before we met, that
I would come. He was told what clothes I would be wearing and
that I was of the advanced bloodline of Quetzacotyl. He also said
other things which can not be written at this time. Quetzacotyl was
a great prophet and ruler of the Mayan civilization and was a previous incarnation of the Master Koothumi. I was one of his family at
that time.

Nityananda also appeared to him at three in the morning a
few days before I arrived. Nityananda, the teacher of Muktananda,
is a great cosmic being and a master of the inner Tantra, who has
become one with certain cosmic doorways of higher initiation.

Virochana is perfect for me in every conceivable way. He is every possible reflection I ever need. The idea of perfection is not something created in the mind. It is an on going meditative experience. We see how our differences complement each other, and bring to the relationship enough stimulation for constant growth. We do not have to agree on every subject (though mostly we do). In our perfection we accept our uniqueness and constantly allow the differences to expand parts of our beingness, for growth. In this way we say we are "perfecting the perfection."

When the ascension of both body and mind is achieved by the Twin Flames they are able to command and control great cosmic activities. The time is near when this mighty Divine wisdom will be demonstrated by the twin rays or Eternal Beloveds upon the earth.

In our first brief meeting I knew this man did not need to heal or learn about relationships with the feminine. He had mastered that long ago! He was the very first man I had ever met who had achieved this mastery, a very rare quality and level of freedom. I also saw at this time that he could have anything he wanted. His purity and awareness showed the vastness of Grace awaiting to be bestowed on him, and the fact that he would never want anything before its ordained timing. When we desire something too quickly we are out of alignment with the "Mother" and enter into struggle.

I have learned much patience and allowance in this area being with Virochana. For the first few days, having been through more years of relationship experiences, I felt he was too pure for me. This was an important healing that I completed with his Love. From the moment we came together we knew we were to stay in each other's auras for at least nine months (never apart for more than two or three hours maximum) and this was also I instructed by the inner Masters, as it was necessary for our fusion.

This Love fusing created dynamic impact in the inner planes, and we could write volumes on the process and interactions that occurred with other beings on the inner, from this world and from other worlds. We were opening every layer of our consciousness to be reflected as a mirror within each other, and within the earth Herself.

It has been because of our commitment to living a conscious life that we have been able to constantly keep growing and cutting through any thought or action which no longer reflects the level of conscious participation that we wish to be a part of, which is the Christ Light. We have had to show our commitment in many different ways with many different people. Our actions are not always understood by others.

Virochana and I enjoyed our "honeymoon" in the jungle at Kipahulu, Maui. We had a twelve by twelve foot cabin with a large loft. The whole structure was screened on three sides, thus making it airy and harboring a conducive feeling to the surroundings. It was our paradise, and he definitely slowed down in his laboring on the farm from the day we met.

I decided we should move on and we left Maui in October 1987, to come to New Zealand. Virochana had never been out of the United States, and the night before we left for New Zealand he was taken above the planet by the Ascended Masters and shown different vibratory vortices of the planet. He was shown how different karmas are being worked out in some areas and where the higher incoming frequency is able to be manifest. This was demonstrated by certain colored lights emitting from within the earth and above it to the surface in certain areas. In all but New Zealand the higher

frequency was limited to small areas. The whole of the country of New Zealand was contained within this higher frequency. We understood the blessings New Zealand holds. It is protected in certain ways, and I am grateful to be born a New Zealander so that we may have ongoing interaction with the spiritual growth of this country. I have also been shown how New Zealand was once part of Lemuria and was the seat of rulership for that civilization. Many souls drawn to New Zealand at this time are old Lemurians being drawn to what they feel as a home where they can feel their pure connection to the earth, an earth that is still strong, vital and relatively unpolluted.

The spiritually awakened state called enlightenment, is what we term clarity, and we believe this is the foundation necessary for creating the new humanity. This clarity is being free of karmic distortions, and is the necessary platform for dynamic change. Few people even believe that enlightenment is possible for them this time around, and do not have the passion of growth. The state of consciousness generally on this planet is one of struggle and resistance. We trust that we will reach out to those souls who want something more, a more refined expansive level of freedom, and happiness, and who have not yet sold their souls to Maya! We say we are here for the Christ initiates and it took us as Twin Rays united in the Oneness, four years of initiations and maturing to put our understandings into a teaching.

On joining we began a great journey of reawakening on many subtle levels. This included facing challenges from numerous fourth and fifth dimensional teachers who base their power in separation. We have realized without doubt LOVE IS THE GREATEST POWER OF THE UNIVERSE. It demands absolute purity, clarity, self honesty, surrender to the Mother. Love has no need of being worshipped or idolized. All teachers on the earth plane who require worshipping and who sit above their students are not, I repeat, are not beings of Love, and are in the bondage of their own karmas.

At the time of meeting Virochana, the Goddess within me was not fully integrated and Goddess was not a word I used in my vocabulary. It was through the Love of the Beloved incarnate, through the ultimate Grace bestowed on us by the Beloved inner

Masters, and through the perfect timing of the Mother, that this integration has occurred. I now stand strongly knowing, I AM the awakened Goddess, serving the ONENESS.

Upon our arrival in New Zealand we stayed initially for a few days with friends whom we enjoyed meditating with. Lana and Richard had two children, one girl and one boy. The girl, six years old, had started to have bad dreams a week before, and was begining to get sick. Lana asked us if we saw anything. Instantly my attention was drawn to some books of a certain world known fifth dimensional teacher. I asked her how long had she had these books - she answered she had been given them about two weeks earlier by a man I also knew. I asked her what else did she have of this teacher. She told me a photo and sacred ash. We knew instantly this was the source of her little girl's disturbance. I said "get rid of these vibrations, call in the protection of the Christ Light and your little girl will be alright."

She did so, and that night as my Beloved and I were sleeping in the caravan we were awakened by an inner battle. I had felt an energy trying to suffocate me and when I woke up on the inner I saw different shapes being formed into a blockade around me. I could feel a band being closed around my Beloved's heart area also. I attempted to maneuver myself beyond the grip of these obstacles and eventually called upon the Masters for help. My Beloved and I both sat up in bed and saw physically twelve beings with long hair hanging upside down in the willow tree by our window looking at us. They were half human, half reptilian. We laughed and we continued meditating.

My Beloved saw quite clearly a vicious red dog's face, and asked, "what is the energy behind this?" He then saw the face of the man who had left the books and ash with our friend, and then the teacher of these books appeared.

He said to my Beloved, "I love you more than anyone does."

Virochana replied, "that's nice, but I've had a long night and I just want to cuddle my Beloved."

This being continued imposing his energy between us. Virochana called on the Ascended Master El Morya and a legion of thousands of beings came to help. There was a confrontation on the inner and my Beloved told this teacher, "never come again in this way." We were free as we had seen through this demonic energy.

This teacher continues to attract thousands of "worshippers and followers," and continues to challenge most people who come to us for guidance. Unless each person is willing to stand alone in their light of the "ONE," they are "prey" to this type of magician.

As an example of another type of magician that we have faced My Beloved was involved all night in a battle with them after one month of our being together.

I observed this also on the inner. Two of these beings we met the following day for the first time, at a place we were thinking to stay at. One of them whom my Beloved had thrown over a ledge on the dream plane, had a swollen ankle and eye. He told us, upon physically meeting, this swelling had come up mysteriously during the night. We understood we did not have to stay at this place. These two men and one other we recognized later as having strong karmic connection from a region in the Sagittarius constellation. We have met a number of these souls and they are all in conflict with their existence on the earth - and try to obtain certain powers through manipulation of the light. Our Love and coming together has enabled us to see many of these types of subtle karmic underplays, hence the reason for these beings challenging us on the inner.

After two weeks in New Zealand we bought a van and started moving. The Mother guided us in New Zealand and elsewhere to particular places on the earth to meditate and unveil past experiences, contained within the earth's karmic cellular memory. This cellular memory is an etheric layer of imprints left in the earth by individual and collective events. These imprints have a timing for clearing and we have found ourselves participating in lifting group karmas into the light of Love and clarity. At times we are instructed to sleep on the earth for a number of months and just surrender to where we are guided day by day to be: completely trusting and letting go, and seeing the perfection of events as the Mother unfolded them to us. We lived out of our van for seven months meditating deeply with the earth in this way.

Recently we have been informed that we hold the respon-
sibilities of a Kumara for the Earth. Our understanding is that there
are forty Kumaras on the Earth working under the direction and
light of Sanat Kumara, BabaJi, and the Planetary Logos who initiate and stimulate the collective release of karmas of humankind.
The Kumaras hold the energetic authority and responsibility to be
present on and work with the crystal energy vertices on the Earth.
The Kumaras are able to clear group karmas, and bring the light of
Grace and understanding on a molecular level into the subconscious
mind of humankind. This is a co-created Grace of the Divine Presence and the growth of souls here on Earth.

In the period of 1987-90 we had many inner revelations
which at times included what are commonly called spaceships and
space beings. These beings we discovered were from a variety of
sources. We were shown spaceships and met beings from Venus,
Pleiades, Antares, Jupiter, Orion, Uranus, and Neptune and we
linked with beings from other systems as well. The forms varied
from human-like to insect and some other projected forms. One
group we call the "wasps" took Virochana onto their ships to show
him a number of humanlike "clones" they were experimenting with.
They had an exact clone of my Beloved (which they would project
in the astral dimensions), and showed him with innocence how they
were trying to gain a deeper understanding of third dimensional
existence. They did not really understand that it could be thought
of as intruding and manipulative to take a form and try to influence
it with various thought projections.

From our experiences we have realized there are forth and fifth
dimensional space beings who are not any more "spiritually" awakened
than human beings. It is untrue to feel that just because a being may
appear in other than physical form they are all "Love and Light." The
forth and fifth dimension also holds its limitations and karmas. Some of
the beings in these dimensions are unruly, aggressive and not aligned
with the "Light" of the "ONENESS Christos Light."

On one of these interactions with space ships we were
sleeping in our van on top of some cliffs over the ocean in a special
vortex of New Zealand, an entry way into the inner earth. This area

has been a site of a crystal temple in Lemuria[2].

On this night as is often the case with Virochana and I, we were having the same experience on the inner. We had been taken aboard a spaceship to a banquet that was held in our honor. As the guests of honor we sat at the head of the table with the commander. He was reminding me of my relationship with him and that we had an agreement for him to have freedom to project himself into my astral/emotional body. Through projecting himself into my astral body he was able to gain certain understandings from my experiences. He had partially ascended on another planet over two-thousand years ago, but needed further completions in the physical, before he could obtain the full ascension. This he hoped to do through my body. He wanted to maintain this alliance as he did not want to take physical embodiment himself. I had become conscious at that time to the degree that I had noticed when he was in my astral field I would become aggressive and tended to push Virochana away. I had seen how this was subtly causing disturbance to me and I told the commander I was no longer willing to have this agreement with him. He was very persistent. He even tried to tell Virochana to go away from me. We both recognized him from Atlantis and a family link with him at that time as Virochana's father. Virochana, with help from an Ascended Master by the name of Baba Siri Chand, was able to see some of the subtle details. I told him he would have to incarnate into the physical to finish his karmas with the earth. He was not happy about this.

I woke quickly, sat upright and opened my eyes. Instantly I saw eight golden disc shaped ships fly over our van and disappear into the ocean below. A second later two reappeared out of the ocean

---

[2] We have come to understand a 'crystal vortex' as an empowered energy center on the earth's surface. The energy is centered inside the matrix of the earth's structure and the crystals within the earth have been masterfully arranged so as to bring the light and understandings from within the earth to the surface. We have been shown how a number of these vortices have been building sites for wonderful temples of knowledge, light, and healing of humankind. Many of these places have had more than one temple built on that location during different cultural epochs. Souls connected to these places and experiences can benefit greatly by physically returning to these sites to reconnect with aspects of themselves. By getting in touch with our unfinished karmas, we are simultaneously moving into the etheric blueprint contained within the earth, which is easily bought to the surface of the mind from within these vortices.

and flew straight up. They were now a silvery white light in color. It was another freeing up for me and a release of an astral karma. I was happy to release this soul, who was based in Venus. Shortly after, he was conceived through a couple we later met, and was born a girl.

Experiences of this nature are helpful yet never have I asked for phenomena. We understand they are given for our greater conscious awakening, when it is the "right time," and when we are prepared spiritually. Therefore we do not advise people to go out looking for space beings or inwardly calling them forth. If you are pure in heart and applying dynamic transformative practises in your life - if it is in your destiny to meet some of your "star" family - you shall in the perfect timing as **ordained** by the "ONENESS..." They shall come to you as they have to us.

Many such exciting experiences happen for us in this way. We have had to learn not to talk too much about the "inner experiences," as for many people experiences of a magical nature become the "goal" of their spiritual pursuits, and ego then gets bigger by becoming "spiritual ego." We found by talking loosely of our experiences, people missed the point of sincere practice and we in fact did them a mis-service.

We are often moving around without knowing where we may be in a week's time, sometimes even daily shifting has been required of us. We understand these times to be what we term earth initiations. In other words, initiations carried out with the support and direction of the Mother's energy. At these times there is no place for analyzing events and trying to control the outer movement from the flow of inner guidance. These are very powerful revelations which test our complete willingness to surrender and trust the Divine plan, under which we grow into alignment in a more conscious way through direct experience.

During these earth initiations each person need understand they are clearing karmas individually and assisting collective awakening. The more conscious One is willing to be, the more "effective" One is. The initiate at these times is also being moulded by the Divine to be able to carry out what teaching and participation will be asked of them. All that one can do under these initiations is to keep up a daily Sadhana of clearing, and strengthening one's commitment to one's Divinity. It will be different in subtle ways for each individual, as the process will differ according to the varied factors in a soul's disposition, environment, karmas, and qualitative tendencies, and the weaknesses to be overcome. It will be different for a person say in New York city and a person in the outback of Australia. The commitment I believe will be the ultimately determining factor. In other words if One is called to go thousands of miles to complete a process, or connect to a new potential, will they go? Each one of us may be asked to answer this type of question at some stage.

In early 1988, My Beloved Virochana and I were called to go to Fiji. This call came through a number of dreams, involving a spiritual teacher living on one of Fiji's smaller islands.

We were at that time travelling in the North Island of New Zealand in our van and sleeping on the earth. We had just enough money for the plane fare and a few hundred dollars. We left New Zealand not certain where we were going, or whom we would meet.

Chapter Twelve

FIJIAN ADVENTURES

*U*pon arrival at Nadi airport we chose between about twenty people promoting the particular hotel or lodge they worked for. The young lady we went with was warm and sincere and we understood from our first night's dreams that we had spiritual sharing with this soul. After a few days she suggested we go to her family's village.

Travelling to the village meant wading across a waist deep river with our bags over our heads and navigating a very muddy track up a steep hill, which for us was amusing and fun. The village people lived in thatched huts with bits of corrugated iron for roofing, very basic, no running water or flush toilets. They lived with maybe six people sharing one small room, and with much kindness we were invited to stay in one such place. The parents, brother and sister of the young Fijian girl at our lodge in Nadi gave us their room and went to sleep next door with relatives. We enjoyed the simple warm ability of these islanders to share easily what little they had, and their trusting, relaxed attitude to life.

On the third night in the village I was bitten by a large centipede, which assisted me in surrendering to the situation, as I was feeling some resistance to being there. Pain has always helped me to go deeper within to see what needs to be healed in my emotional (astral) etheric field. The centipedes poison in this sense acted as a stimulant to bring up vividly my images and thoughts of resistance. Virochana was shown in dreams, for three consecutive nights, a house which we understood was connected to our next step. After informing our hosts that we preferred to live in quietude and simple natural surroundings they arranged for us to travel to an outlying island and be met by their relatives.

Before leaving the village for this island, Virochana had several visions and dreams whereby he defeated a fifth dimensional demonic influence that had inadvertently brought about the deaths of seventeen of the villagers. The word visions perhaps does not give the sense of strength, depth, and reality of these interactions, which have the force of moving physical objects, and influence many lives. We also had strong dream interaction and transmissions with some of the spiritual elements in Fiji.

The island we travelled to was very beautiful with very little development and few tourists. It suited us well, and we were given the opportunity to stay in the house which my Beloved had seen in dream-time, two hundred feet up on a hill overlooking the brilliant blue sparkling ocean.

Over the next few months we shared this large run down home with a happy fijian couple who were managing the 200 acre unproductive copra plantation. We scrubbed down a room, and Virochana made a makeshift bed, and fixed the window screens. They left us to our meditations, and accommodated us in a genu-inely warm friendly way[1]. We ate what they ate in the way of local fruits and vegetables, but not the refined foods and meats and fish. Nothing was as we could have imagined. It is always wise not to have expectations when entering into new situations. The time spent here gave us plenty of opportunity to demonstrate a life of ease without expectations, with much meditation. At times the air was very still, hot and humid, and there was little outside stimulation.

The snorkeling was magnificent, with the rainbow colors of fish and coral, and it was our almost daily form of exercise and enjoyment. Our inner astral work was vivid and full of prophecies, instruction, and revelations. Here we did a lot of astral clearing of

---

[1] While not without their problems, these simple and relaxed people were quiet and at peace with the earth and their life, living simply without modern appliances, TV, etc.

karmas and saw parts of the bigger picture involving many beings that was being played out. We saw how introduced cultural, religious, and political structures had imposed great limitations on these warm friendly people, and how this paradise was incomplete, due to their lack of Self understanding. These island people have been heavily indoctrinated by the Christian missionaries. This indoctrination was an attempt to change these people's beliefs, some of which needed change, especially the violence of cannibalism which was still practised at the time the missionaries came to the islands. The indoctrination that has stifled these people's growth by presenting half truths was very noticeable to us. They do not think for themselves, in many areas, rather they rely heavily on the church and the chiefs to tell them how to behave. Nothing is by accident, and the introduction of additional cultural limitations from outside sources is a reflection of collective and individual seeds of disharmony and ignorance of Divine laws already present within any native culture.

The spiritual teacher who had called us was unavailable to us, as the religious structure around him made it impossible to have physical contact. We were told by the priests we would have to join the organization as devotees and do worship maybe one year before being "granted" an audience! This we found arrogant and silly. We did however continue much interaction with him in our light bodies on the inner planes. He has established an organization around himself of devotees who worship him as their saviour. We cannot align to this energy, as we know it to be an incomplete and disempowering spiritual expression. I also came to see over the next two years how I was completing some karmas with this Teacher from previous incarnations. It was fortunate that I completed this on an astral level, rather than be drawn into his dominating physical manipulative influence.

Wanting to help the local people in a cooperative venture, we decided to start a viable, environmentally sound, economically prosperous venture, processing some of the local organic fruits which we would dry and export. As most of the fruit was rotting on the island, with no market, it seemed like a positive idea. We knew that if the universe wished it to happen we would be given clear guidance.

Over one month the idea grew inside us, and at this time we were guided to two men whom we felt were suitable to start the business with. They were both local, one having been in Australia for a short time, and the other having lost his paid job when he was called back to this island after his wife had left him. This man, Arthur, had six children and could barely afford to send them to school clothed, fed, and equipped with books etc. Though we shared very little of our spiritual practices with them, they responded with the sincere, honest, practical qualities we all needed to get this venture off the ground. It seemed beside the point that we were on our last few dollars, with no way to renew our visas, and with no clear understanding of how the funds would manifest. In fact we did not even have a return air ticket as they had been sent back for a refund. We had already total faith in the workings of the universe, and were clear on the pure intention of our proposed project.

Three days before our visas expired, my brother with his family, including Sunjaya, happened to be passing through Fiji on holiday and he sent a telegram saying they would like to meet with us. The miracle we needed happened and we used our last dollars to get a series of planes to the main island, and then a taxi ride across the island to the hotel where my family was staying. We assured our island friends we would return with all the necessary funds in the near future. Arthur never doubted us, the others were not so sure. My brother paid our taxi fare, gave Virochana one-hundred dollars, and sat us down to a four-hundred dollar meal in a luxury hotel. We went from poverty, searching the jungles for food, to excess in a few hours. My brother and sister in law graciously paid our expenses over the next few days. It was a healing reunion and wonderful for me to see Sunjaya again, who was by now almost fifteen years of age.

After putting the proposal of the dried fruit company to my brother, he gave us air tickets and funds to fly to Australia. He agreed Virochana should research the idea, and put it into motion if it looked good. This was totally amazing to me, as my brother and his sister-in-law had for a long time doubted my sanity, in pursuing what they saw as a worthless existence without any ambition. They liked my Beloved. Little did they know of the depths of growth I had achieved over the past fourteen years, and how that was all to serve me in the future.

During the first two months in Australia, Virochana put together a comprehensive business plan to present to investors. During this time we overcame many obstacles, by holding close our vision and belief in what we intended to do. When it came to securing funds, I picked up the phone book and started intuitively calling phone numbers from the yellow pages of people whom I felt may be suitable investors. We miraculously drew together all the money needed in the following few weeks, after meeting with about six people. We returned quickly to Fiji.

Here in Suva we had our company incorporated and got necessary approval from the government to begin business. Happily we returned to our home island and everyone was elated to see our initial success and our presence was greatly welcomed. There were a few preliminary signs of undercurrents at work, such as our plane almost crashing upon landing. Later, on the day of our incorporation, the plane did crash. While there were injuries, luckily no-one was killed.

Because we now had working funds, we rented an unused very comfortable furnished european style home. In this large development there were several dozen homes that had been built for Europeans as holiday residences, all having much unused land around them. This whole development had gone bankrupt, and many people had homes but no legal title to the land they were built on, and could not sell them, or get extended visas to live in them. In this developed section all the roads are paved and the landscaped properties are all uninhabited, while the locals just next door are without paved roads or running water or any modern conveniences. We could not help but feel that the bankruptcy was some kind of justice being played out, as most of this development had been funded by drug money. This we were told by one local man who managed the care-taking and occasional rental.

We became very aware of how outside people often see these Pacific islands and other economically undeveloped regions as easy pickings. Cheap labor in paradise, and then insensitive development to exploit the natural resources so that a few wealthy, indulgent tourists can have all their extravagant needs attended to.

On our island we were informed that the land on which we were planning to build our factory had been taken, with the local chief's approval, by a Korean company. This company had just proposed to come in and log the largest remaining rainforest in the area, against the advice of the government's forestry and conservation departments. They also intended to blast the beautiful coral reefs, to create a yacht marina, and build a mill for a local food product.

We asked our friends, who by this time were employees helping to assemble the dryers, to find us another suitable piece of land for the dried fruit factory, and we wrote some letters to government. These stated that we saw the move of the Korean company as one which would not in any way benefit the local environment, and therefore people. A large proportion of these people had never seen widespread logging.

Many of these simple people could not imagine the type of people who would exploit an environment for greed to the ultimate detriment of a whole society. They trusted whatever their chief would say, and blindly followed hierarchical opinion. So it was that we entered more deeply into the lives of these people.

Energetically we went about building our dryers, experimenting with drying a variety of fruits, and bringing in everything we needed. I had a growing persistent feeling by this time that we would not succeed, and upon sharing this with my Beloved I realized He was so determined to succeed that he could not hear me. I would get upset but it made no difference and so we went through the motions of getting this business under way.

It was our intention that when it was operating we would leave the business mostly in the hands of our employees. We had three Fijian men in mind at this stage. There were also a number of local farmers with plenty of fruits available, and we made agreements as to how much fruit we would need. It was planned that, as we became successful, we would buy land, put it into trust, and start a spiritually based teaching community. As time went on we became aware of all the resistance that was beginning to surface. We saw petty jealousies between families, and saw how one of them could not get ahead materially without incurring difficulties for themselves from the others. There was discord over whose land we should have for building, and after two different ideas, one of our employees offered us his plot, but his relatives were not happy.

We went to meet the island's chief as we were informed we needed his blessing. After that meeting we began to hear rumors about us and upon inquiry we found out it was coming from the chief. We went again to see him and we were reluctantly informed that he would fix everything up for us. He had a strong prejudiced dislike of the Fijian Indians. We have an Indian surname from which he equated we would favor Indians in our business. The chief, by the way, was also the president of Fiji.

We did not realize at this time that the chief expected a tithe (bribe) from our company, as this was the usual practise, and was unhappy that we did not play the game. We were really naive to the undercurrents, and our Fijian friends were out of their depth.

Around this time my Beloved broke out in bloody-type sores on his back that caused him much discomfort, and a local healer came to see him and told us our enemies had put a death curse on us and that he could die. We responded by sitting in meditation and asking that the energy be returned from where it came. I was given a powerful revelation on the inner during sleep regarding the fifth dimensional source of this type of energy. The source of the energy came from Uranus, and was a misuse of the red, yellow, and violet rays. We have met a number of souls grounding this type of karma on earth. In this particular case there were also karmic overtones of the Orion energy. We were informed several weeks later by the acting prime minister, that on the day we returned the energy the government official who was responsible for stopping our work permits had gone into the hospital with a heart attack. Coincidence? I think not. For us there is no such thing as coincidence, just the conscious working out of spiritual and natural laws.

One of our employees informed us he had just found out a local man (whom we never met) had been given three thousand dollars to harass our operations. The chief had ordered the revoking of our work permits, and as he had a top Government position he was obeyed. We were exposed to how these men and others, were responsible for inciting the native Fijians against the Indian community. This was to create a diversion, so that corrupt politics would not be exposed. This enabled certain men to stay in power politically. Three million dollars was also received by the chief from a Korean company in return for their favors in securing land and favorable arrangements. Some of this was openly stated in the local newspaper. Just what some call a "normal" business deal. Additional information was revealed to us by locals and people within government workings including one of Fiji's principle lawyers.

To gain a better idea of the state of affairs, it was against the law to print anything in the newspapers which might be judged as opposed to the stability of the country, as determined by the leaders.

Our work permits were revoked, and Visas set to expire shortly. Upon contacting top government officials (including the president) it was stated that it was all a misunderstanding on their part, and that it would be taken care of. However untrue rumors were started on the island, and our investigation eventually revealed that they were spread by certain government officials as part of certain power plays. Our permits remained revoked. We were not informed of this and it was only through my persistent ringing of a government official that I found this out. I was then informed we had three days to leave Fiji!, I said "your government has already given us permission to carry out business on the island." The official replied "the top official and chief you have come up against is the government." I then replied "Well, you have a corrupt government." To which he replied "Mrs. Khalsa, you are out of here," and that was the end of that. One of our Fijian friends (who was a well-respected member of the community as a Justice of the Peace) and two police officials with angelic names arrived at our home a half-hour later. They told us they had been sent to tell us to leave. They were very upset by the whole ordeal and the captain said "even if our chief is corrupt, we never say so." I said "I could never live like that," and felt relieved to be leaving." We went to the main island after only a few hours to pack to meet with senior members of the government. They examined our complaint for the possibility of bringing a court case against these unscrupulous beings, but they just did not have the strength, and they advised us to leave. We met other government officials who were all embarrassed and very sorry for what had happened.

Our factory was just beginning to be built, and we had a newly built boat to collect fruits. We had a working temporary building, and all the equipment was shared around the local people. Two tons of fruit were given away and boxes of premium organic dried fruit eaten by many locals for no cost. We were unable to return to salvage anything, and our friends cried as we left. Two hundred local farmers signed a petition in four hours requesting that we be able to stay, this was shown to government officials, but to no avail.

We left after having spent 30,000 dollars. At the time we left, an article appeared in the newspaper reporting a UFO that was seen in broad daylight by many people sitting above the island (we knew we were getting much etheric observation).

The bloody sores on Virochana's back started to disappear as soon as we left Fiji (literally on the aeroplane after leaving Fijian airspace). Within a week they were totally gone. We came to understand that this experience for him was as karmic completion of past-life confrontations with a particular group of approximately eighty-two souls that had in the past led my Beloved into self doubt through their judgements. The man who had revoked our permits in Fiji and had gone to hospital was one of these eighty-two souls. Because of past actions that still tied Virochana to self defensiveness, the energy of psychic attack was able to penetrate his auric field.

From this experience he better understood how this Karma was created, and after another incident yet to come, released himself totally from this type of interaction. This experience showed us many things about the state of the world condition, and the injustices that are allowed to occur daily. We had got caught up in someone else's mess, and had neither the support, nor the time, to improve the overall situation.

We have since been informed that the logging has commenced on this fragile land, despite protest from Fiji's Minister in charge of forestation.

This experience and subsequent understandings assisted us to realize that our true, most required function on the planet at this time is the role of spiritual teachers.

Chapter Thirteen

SPIRITUAL ENTRAPMENTS OF THE WOMAN DEVOTEE - MALE GURU RELATIONSHIP

*M*any times over the past twenty years I have seen women demonstrating a particular limitation when entering the spiritual path under a male Guru, which needs addressing from a conscious viewpoint.

Most of us enter into spiritual teachings looking to fill the gap of incompleteness in our lives. This incompleteness may be due to needing answers to deep pressing questions regarding the meaning of life, or the search for happiness and desire to find true LOVE... Often lack of fulfilled love drives a soul to turn to religious understandings in the hope of finding fulfillment. In our materialistic society many people have realized that money and material possessions do not buy happiness - hence the next step is to find spiritual answers that give peace to the soul.

The unhappiness that exists in the arena of sexual relationship is widespread and common. Most women have never developed the ability to enter into deep intimate communion with a tantric consort[1]. As a result of little spiritual understanding and lack of Self Love, looking for that "LOVE" in another, they continually experience unfulfilling relationships.

---

[1] Tantric Consort - an advanced yogi partner of the opposite sex, with whom one is able to actively and harmoniously transmute energy into a refined enlightened condition.

With this underlying unhappiness they begin seeking spiritual answers and are often drawn into a Guru-devotee relationship and transfer all these unexpressed emotions towards the Male Guru. This unconscious reaction to their inner state of unfulfilled Love becomes directed towards worshipping the form of the "perfect" Guru who holds for them the fantasy of the perfect relationship.

Holding onto this "ideal man" is of course quite safe as the Guru is usually far from reach in an intimate way and the fantasy of the "perfect" male can be played out, without confrontational intimate emotional exchange. In reality it is dependency addiction transferred to yet another relationship. Even if the Guru becomes sexually available, these men are already well schooled in how to maintain a hierarchical "top" position, and will happily reinforce or exploit the vulnerability of their devotees, females and males. This is the Guru-Devotee mentality.

I have seen many examples and read many books that continue to idolize this Guru-devotee relationship. My nature being very emotional and feminine is naturally a Bhakti (devotional) disposition. In this I was lead at a young age into the arms of my first teacher in India, a very advanced Tantric Yogi who was blessedly happy with his wife and family. Fortunately for him she was probably his twin ray, therefore he was totally fulfilled. Fortunately for me I had the destiny to be freed quickly of my looking for LOVE and fulfillment outside myself.

I have since come to see what an incredibly precious gift I obtained on the beginning of my searching for Self.

Most are not this fortunate, and the disempowered abused feminine energy is a great dis-ease on planet earth. I have often been involved in and had to pass through these karmic scenarios and I have observed other woman trapped in them. Having witnessed many male Gurus in action I now speak strongly and clearly on this subject - wanting to help other women and men get free.

I have seen this worshipping of a male Guru occurring frequently with women in unfulfilled marriages, and the husband takes second place to the "God" like Guru. In truth this is never satisfying to the husband, and the beauty of real intimate relationship carried out in a conscious tantric discipline is never brought to fruition. For any relationship to be fulfilling, it must promote dynamic growth. If one maintains a wife and husband relationship, it should be from a sense of total fulfillment, and freedom on every level. Staying in a marriage of "convenience" never brings happiness and often blocks any worthwhile growth in both parties. People use each other in this way to remain at a comfortable level of physical and material security.

We must realize that we have to be free from role playing, we must set ourselves and loved ones free, to have the clarity to address all our deeper unresolved issues. Otherwise relationships remain as another form of escape from our True Self (Oneness) and neurosis is perpetuated.

This emotional and spiritual neediness also feeds these manipulative Gurus, who usually take the stance of a celibate (if not happily married) whilst constantly emitting their magnetism as subtle seduction for unsuspecting females. There are also instances of these Gurus, whom I shall not name, being sexually involved with some of their favored female devotees, yet outwardly lying about it. These men have a long way to go for their own healing. They also continue to create and perpetuate many karmas - and it is a long journey ahead for their eventual attainment of the ascended body.

The Beloved Ascended Masters have long since completed these karmas - and never, never allow themselves to be worshipped by anyone!! It is an insult to the Divinity of each being!!

The Guru and devotees entrapped in these karmas often create an organization with many rules which includes an extreme display of devotional[2] attitudes by their devotees, such as being worshipped with garlands of flowers and the performance of pujas[3].

---

[2] Devotional - A praise filled attitude is a natural expression arising from the longing heart in every spiritually evolved being. Unfortunately it is greatly misrepresented and misused on this Earth.

[3] Puja - A religious ceremony in which a devotee invokes the Divine presence by paying homage to a photo or statue or living being that is looked upon as holy. This is done with candles, incense, and usually the chemistry of a holy song or mantra.

This devotional display is what I have passed through and come to realize as a purification and opening of the fourth chakra - the heart - through which spiritual truths may be grasped. In this state of vulnerability a devotee is easily exploited by those slightly more experienced souls still needing to be worshipped.

It is easy to take someone's light by getting them to focus on you and making them emotionally dependent. Until a soul realizes the "Light" as being within themselves there is often an emotional need to worship the "light" through another called "Guru." WHAT OFTEN HAPPENS IS THAT THE "GURU" FALLS TO SPIRITUAL EGO AS THEY STILL HAVE KARMAS NOT YET DEALT WITH AND "THINK" THEMSELVES AS THE "LIGHT" OF OTHERS, RATHER THAN A FINGER TO POINT TO THE LIGHT INSIDE EVERY PERSON. Any teacher that claims exclusive rights to the highest teachings such as being "The World Saviour," "The Only True Messenger," etc., is deluded.

My advice is that if you see this possessive, controlling undercurrent in a spiritual teacher's stance - avoid these beings, they are trouble. This type of Guru is not totally enlightened and is unfulfilled emotionally to some degree. Virochana and I have come to understand that the Tantric path which is the embrace of form requires absolute purity. Tantra requires a deep solid foundation of disciplined practise and humility. These Gurus of devotees are on a tantric path. On the Tantric path there are only two outcomes. One either becomes a monster or they become a Buddha. A Buddha is free on all levels including the need of organization and followers. Those Gurus caught in this type of karmic entrapment have not received the ultimate blessing of the Divine Mother. This ultimate blessing is the coming together with one's Eternal Beloved Twin Ray. Being with one's Twin Ray automatically establishes a balanced true relationship with all beings and the Earth's providence.

Again being with Virochana has given me a clear perspective from which to address this issue and serve the Mother's desire for the Goddess (energy) to awaken.

The devotee mentality comes from a lack of Self empowerment, and in the need for "worshipping a Guru," rather than focusing on the reasons why Self empowerment does not exist. Otherwise the focus is on worshipping the light of the Guru who needs to be worshipped. This may give a person temporary solace in the illusion that they are being "saved" by the Guru, but in the long term unhappiness comes as a result of giving away One's own power and not acknowledging the Light within Oneself.

These devotee women are not addressing their self-created limitations and constantly project their problems as outside themselves. Often they feel there are no men worth entering deep honest relationships with - rather than seeing it as their own limitation, and holding the "enlightened guru" as the fantasy.

Unfulfillment within any relationship is a result of personal unfulfillment through not realizing oneSelf as "Divine." When we enter into relationships of a sexual nature from an unfulfilled state, which of course can never be filled by one's partner, we create much subconscious anger. This anger when directed towards the male energy sets in motion a cycle of unfulfillment with feelings of recurring rejection. Fulfillment and happiness is found when we awaken the truth of our own Divinity. We can then free ourselves of all karmic constricting relationships, and are able to free others into becoming the God/Goddess whom we are in truth. This is a teaching whose time has come.

To clarify the reality that a teacher is required, I would like to state that it is absolutely necessary that the process of purification and elimination of the separative state be entered into. For a time this purification will require celibacy, and will require the vital guidance of a spiritual teacher. The type of teacher you are attracted to will be a direct reflection of your own karmas and purity. So you may grow through many teachers, or you may instantly have one that you can go all the way with. This is all as a result of past actions.

Do not judge anyone's path. The duration of celibacy and purification and strengthening is different for each soul. Only a free, happy, and emotionally fulfilled teacher can clearly see the right timing for each person and guide them skilfully, without any underlying tendency to bind that soul to them personally.

Once surrendered and under the powerful influence of one's teacher, it is very difficult for a novice to objectively see all that is going on personally for their teacher. Everyone likes to believe that "Their Guru" is perfect, and is naturally reluctant to accept anyone else's observations. As you become clear and light, more and more is understood.

It is the awakened feminine, "The Goddess," that has the power to change men into what the Goddess and Mother requires. The awakened Goddess will bring forth the new man, the awakened God. This is what is being asked of women as they regain their inner light of ONENESS.

This inherent inner power of the feminine principle is One with Divine Mother. Our great Divine Mother is all of creation, she cannot be avoided, suppressed, or dominated. Every being must eventually surrender to the Mother to gain the fruits of their endeavors. She alone gives happiness and fulfillment on earth. She is beyond technique, beyond action, and without Her Grace no one can feel peace on Earth.

To experience this as I have, a woman must first experience her body as the Divine earth. She must be free of weakening self doubt, insecurities, and materialistic attitudes. The "Way of the Goddess" is essentially a call to women to purify, strengthen, and awaken their Divine Essence. This empowerment of the feminine principle will bring forth integrated knowingness of one's highest purpose in creation.

These light, happy and free women will bring honor back to the Goddess, demonstrating their attunement to the earth's wishes and their power to change the tide of self destruction which engulfs our earth presently.

The light, happy and free Goddess can then truly assist in the healing of men.

Chapter Fourteen

INTEGRATING EARTH'S NEW FREQUENCY

*E*arly in 1989, three weeks after leaving Fiji, we received a letter from a friend inviting us to go to the island of Kauai in Hawaii and participate in the formation of a spiritual community.

The necessity to share consciously and co-create new model communities of a harmonious and enlightened nature is something we see as a vital step towards bringing individual and collective balance to this earth. Conscious co-creation in this way is indeed a step towards our planetary, and therefore individual, joy filled coexistence. Virochana and I are committed to participation in bringing through these centers of Light for happy and free beings.

Materialism has shown us how struggle is increased with more desires (greed) and the goal of materialism is always to want more, ever eluding fulfillment. From materialistic attitudes, we have co-created an unfulfilled society. This has further caused an increase of drugs, broken homes, disease, poverty (which is a reflection of those who have more than they need), violent media productions, rebellious children, climate and atmospheric disruptions, government's unsolvable debt problems, etc., etc.

All these issues are painfully obvious and are now gaining more honest attention. We as humanity can no longer pretend we are on the "right" track. This is why the "new age" awareness is expanding with increasing numbers of people seeking answers and alternatives to the present status quo.

Lack of caring, of conscious attunement, and of inter-connected supportive activities, have driven people to stress, disease and despair. The earth reflects this suffering. It is an affront to the Oneness which we are, and to the Mother who nourishes us all.

We decided to go to Hawaii and see what was happening there. We love Hawaii's softness and climate and have come to understand that Hawaii is a major planetary vortex for the blend-ing and dissemination of the "New Age," and the teachers of "ONENESS." We call the island of Maui the "heart" of the "New World." As a major planetary vortex, Hawaii attracts many souls who want to heal their feminine energies, and who sincerely want to grow in spiritual understanding. Much healing of relationships and emotions is available through the "Mother's" energy on these beautiful islands. Hawaii also attracts people seeking power who consciously and semi-consciously manipulate the "pure light." The island of Kauai we experienced as a major vortex which has direct access into the entire crystal grid system of the planet. It is a place where anyone can consciously clear any karmic imprint from their history on the planet. Kauai has been the site of many mystery schools in the past. We now call them mastery schools and call Kauai the island of high initiations. Beings who wish to manipulate the light of others are in great numbers in Hawaii and have created a strong unruly disruptive psychic field of influence. We see these unruly forces as ultimately serving the "light" and our purpose, as they help to polarize the energies and gradually people are making powerful choices, as to what it is they wish to align to right now!!

Our requirement to align with others, is that they are will-ing and able to stand in their own inner Light. This Light being the Light of the ONE. Here in the Oneness there is no conflict that arises out of dualistic states of awareness.

The people we met in Kauai were still in the individual healing stage and there was not then a happy, working cohesive group project. The idealism was being "talked" about - but the change necessary to co-create a model community of the ONENESS was only happening on the visionary level.

The inner work to align oneself to the "ONE" has no short cuts and we realized it was in the future still for the collective manifestations of clear free beings, and these enlightened communities of the new frequency. We know the timing of the earth is all-important and a number of souls at this time have seen the co-created vision for the next step of a healed humanity. Many are in the process of healing as the need for Oneness grows more and more urgent. This requires constant diligence to purify, to act purely, and to surrender simultaneously. The majority of these people see themselves as "healers" and are involved in their own form of Self healing, which may take many years. We cannot push the ordained sequence of events that must be fulfilled before we, as a collective, move into the new frequency of a clear humanity.

Virochana and I knew we must go our way and allow each person their experiences. We were enjoying being, and strengthening together. We were in Love, simply content. We were directed internally to sleep on the earth, stay contained in our meditations, and trust the inner process. A tent was given to us and we bought a car which Virochana payed for through part time work.

We were guided through what was shown to us as the eighth through twelfth level initiations. Virochana saw one night above our tent a large neon sign flashing the words eighth level initiations, and a voice from everywhere said you are now entering eighth level initiations. How much more graphic can you get! We were having

much visual and telepathic contact on the inner with Pleiadean beings, some Assasani beings, the Beloved Ascended Masters, and
Yogi Bhajan. The teachings were profound and unlocked a number
of inner masteries to us. Such a joy, such a blessing!

Every day unfolded the outer play of the inner workings,
and we faced a number of difficult, and interesting situations with
other people. We had developed a sharp ability to connect to a
person's very core and limiting issues. Our mere presence began
to have impact, and trigger off much unresolved karmic cellular
memory. Another less polite word for this is a person's neurosis.

Healings of very deep issues occurred for both of us, and
we were able to cleanse ourselves almost daily in the wonderful
element of water, which we have found to be invaluable during
intense times of inner activation.

Another reason why the water element was invaluable for
us at this time was because it was needed to bring us back everyday
into our physical bodies. We were in the etheric/formless realms
for many hours on end and it was more difficult to be strong in the
physical. It takes a good deal of strength and practice to travel in
ones light body out of the physical body, and water is a blissful element for transition back into the physical. (This is why float tanks
and water rebirthing are beneficial therapies for mind/emotional
expansion). It is also becoming well known that water births for babies
are the most natural and painless way for both mother and baby.

It is my belief that within a few decades we shall acknowledge this by making it available to every woman. If I ever have
another child it will be birthed in water - preferably with dolphins.

It was as a result of our higher initiations and subsequent
awakenings that I was called to bring all of who I Am In Truth onto
the Earth. To totally incarnate into my body to hold this light of
liberation and serve the Mother.

Our bodies are the blueprint for the higher frequencies
being released and activated on the planet at this time. Those of
us who are part of the blueprint are developing a stronger unique
signature matrix through which we can communicate and identify
beyond physical senses.

It is the responsibility of each one of us to strengthen our own unique signature matrix so that we do not become overpowered by the higher frequency - and can participate in the blending of the Higher Tantras.

To empower this blueprint, our left side, our intuitive feminine nature, must be completely clear and unblocked. This is all part of what is called empowering the feminine principle at this time. This activation is simultaneously occurring in the collective embodiment within the seed atoms in this planet, yet it is the beings on the surface through their active commitment that embody this awakening.

We came to realize that very few beings are more than 25% in their bodies. This incarnating fully is the Christing. Bringing the Christ light into the body means simultaneously releasing all karmic cellular memory from one's cells. We call this the stage of descension. Here we experienced descending our bodies as pure light into physicality.

I have experienced the spin of my DNA reversing and my blood being totally cleansed. At the same time as this, I became aware of all the issues of limitation that I was now able to transcend. This change of the flow of my DNA meant for me that I had overcome all my genetic heritage and the ties that perpetuate established realities of my ancestors. I have overcome the ingrained patterns in my DNA that carried thoughts such as disease and death of the body. I knew then I need not ever age this body and had made the choice to be immortal!!

This Grace came about for us because of the Love that flows with the Beloved incarnate and the wanting to be perfect twenty-four hours a day to experience that LOVE without any resistance.

In Kauai at this time I acknowledged the fully conscious blending with Tara. I subsequently added Ra to my name which had been Shanta. I understood this as the completion of integrating and actioning my Solar (male) and Inner-Earth (female) in alignment with my Central Sun Eternal Essence. Shantara is the seventh name I have had on my journey of awakening. Each name carries a vibratory frequency and I enjoyed all my names as I integrated them! Often I offer new names to people who come our way. These new names are the frequency I see them being able to integrate at that time, if they apply themselves dynamically to spiritual disciplines.

Knowing mySelf as the Goddess embodying the qualities and the essence of the Goddess Tara, happened as a result of my diligent practice, being immersed in the Love of the Beloved, and the Grace of the Oneness. All this has been absolutely necessary for my awakening.

"**Ma**" was added to my name after I was given the spiritual blessing and title of a Swami - by the Great Yogi/Saint Paramahansa Yogananda, who came on the inner during sleep and gave me this ordination in early 1991. He said I was the first woman to be ordained as a Swami of the "GIRI" order. I carry the ordination of this Kriya lineage from my previous embodiments.

It is more an inner acknowledgment at this time rather than an outer role, for I do not wear the ochre robes of a swami. I prefer wearing outwardly whatever color feels right in the moment, and belong to no organization.

In 1987 I received full contact on the inner planes with the Eternal Master Beloved Maha Avatar BabaJi who heads this Kriya lineage. This occurred within a week of being united with Virochana. His first words were that now he could make himself visible to me as I was with my Beloved. If he had appeared sooner he said I would have given some of my power to him in my great Love for him. He showed me at that time how I had been with him as a student in my most recent embodiment, in India, and how I had achieved a partially ascended body. He showed me the body I had left in a cave when I transited out of physicality. I had seen this body with Virochana's help and realized why in this embodiment I most often felt I was living on a mountain top. I had left that body as a beacon to tune into when I took this present body to help me maintain inner knowingness of my Divine Essence. This was of great help to me for I embodied into a situation where I could overcome all my previously undealt with accumulated karmas. As I became more aware of it, the lifeforce in my body in the cave began to stir, and again required small bits of nourishment and attention.

MahaAvatar informed me that I could now dissolve the

lifeforce of my suspended yogic body into my present embodiment. That yogic body had completed its purpose to assist me, and I was now conscious enough to integrate fully the wisdom of that body. This I did over a period of a few days. MahaAvatar is my Param Sat Guru (Great embodiment of the elevating Light of Truth) and Beloved Brother. He comes on the inner when necessary to assist ourselves or others.

As the descension of the Christed Self came through more consciously and completely, we saw how it is essential for what we term clearing the five bodies. Acknowledging these five bodies as the physical, emotional, etheric, mental and eternal light monadic body, we have seen that the integration of these are in fact the complete Christing into the physical. Our cellular matrix became literally transformed or transmuted[1] into the Christ light, or the Oneness, and we are beyond any doubt reborn into our eternalness.

From this alignment anyone can regenerate the physical body. This is the willingness to daily live life in a total and conscious way. To be able to maintain the voltage and enthusiasm of a daily joyous positive vibrant life is a great achievement. If any undealt with karmas still remain, often what happens in an uplifting experience is that the experience is followed by a downward pull back into gravity, and further processing.

[1] Transmute - the activity of elevating self and environment which brings about transformation.

Every day on Kauai was one of revelation on the inner, and frequent challenges on the outer. We were shown our individual and collective karmic issues and enjoyed much integration. We became mirrors of these collective karmas and often when we met someone our mere presence stimulated a subconscious response to those activations we were bringing forth. Often people we met were not ready and willing to go into the depth of healing necessary - and retaliated by attempting to block us in some way.

In one of these instances we met a dear sister at an informal sharing we gave one evening to about twelve people.

This sister whom I shall call "Harmony" was one of a group of women I remember teaching in Atlantis. These Women were known as the Crystal priestesses, and all carry similar pain regarding the abuse of the feminine, the abuse of the earth, and the domination of the male priesthood. Harmony was overweight, very sensitive and psychic, always trying to help people, and in denial over the depth of her pain. She always had a happy, helpful outer demeanor and a tremendous power to influence others. I immediately felt great Love for her and knew we were to help her in her healing. She was renting a home, and rented out two extra rooms to tenants that changed every month. These tenants had difficulty living with Harmony as she had a way of getting too involved with everyone's life. This caused her and others much anxiety.

We suggested she leave her home and go and live on the beaches for a while. We were living on the beaches at this time and knew what a healing, peaceful, and freeing experience it was. She began camping on one of Kauai's large beautiful beaches and swimming with dolphins. She started to mellow out a bit, and spend more time with the "Mother" for healing. Many people just could not integrate Harmony's energy and trouble was always nearby her. One morning we went down to see her and she suggested we should meet a young man I will call Miguel who was from Columbia, who had come to stay for a while on Kauai. He was camping on the same beach as Harmony.

Two days later we met Miguel - a young very handsome man with a strong yet refined body. I saw instantly his resemblance

to a great Yogi called Meher Baba who passed from this earth somewhere around the 1940's. We both saw this young man was a soul
with great potential spiritually, who needed to be helped back onto
the path. Miguel was a skilled mime artist and had studied in Paris.
He had also been under the guidance of dark sorcerers in Columbia
and carried this influence still. We told him we could teach him some
Kriyas and Yoga but that he must stop smoking marijuana first.

We knew he wanted to spend time with us, so we invited
him to come and sleep with us in a cave that was special. That night
he kept on touching my arm and hand. At first I thought he was in-
nocently wanting to feel close to me, but when it persisted I began
feeling uncomfortable. Virochana felt it and sat up and told Miguel
to stop it. The next day we all went to see some new friends that
had invited Virochana and I to stay in the condominium they were
renting for ten days. After a shared meal Miguel left and that night
I woke feverish and needing to vomit. My Beloved and Harmony
who was there after insisting she stay the night, told me to get in
touch with the reason I felt sick. As I sat in meditation instantly I
saw Miguel, he had tied me with ropes to a tree. I saw how he was
trying to draw on my light to possess me. I returned the energy,
freeing the ropes and saying "you are only binding yourself." I saw
how the negative influence of the sorcerer was riding on his astral
body. Harmony said she felt Miguel wanted to psychically kill me
as he felt rejected. She wanted to do an exorcism and I allowed
her to bathe me, chant some mantras and light candles and incense
to purify the room of this negative influence. What I saw would
be necessary to free myself fully from this type of intrusion, was
greater clarity. I became aware of how ice-cream and chocolate
created a film over my inner vision and made the decision not to
eat these foods again. One month later when I tasted ice-cream again
instantly my vision blurred and I was happy never to touch it again.

Food, like thoughts, carries vibrational frequencies and we
have stopped eating many foods that people generally eat.

Virochana and I knew that Miguel would have to go through
many more learning experiences before he would elevate himself
out of some of his karmas. We saw him briefly only on a couple

more occasions and Virochana shared with him some of the things he would have to go through - and what he needed to give up, to be able to stay on the spiritual path. Virochana was asked on the inner by some Yogis, not to cast this soul aside despite his psychic attack. They were holding a promise for him to elevate certain group karmas prevalent to a certain star system.

One of our more pleasant experiences on Kauai involved a young ten year old girl, I shall call Malena. Malena was one of two daughters of a dear brother and sister couple we met. This family allowed us to put our tent up on their lawn when we needed a retreat from the beach and other activation points on the island. Malena is outwardly deaf and mute from birth. She is very delicate, slender and highly strung. The second night we camped in their backyard, both Virochana and I were shown revelations concerning this soul. I was taken aboard a Pleiadean ship and told by a council of beings this young girl was embodied for the first time as a human - She was from the Devic/Angelic realm and was too sensitive to hear the grossness of most beings' speech. I was told she was a very highly evolved being who would only speak when enough people were ready to hear what she had to say. I was also told she knew what she needed and should be given all the things she required to stay in her human body. Virochana was told her name was Devaki, and we had to pass through much collective resistance that did not want this connection between Melena and us to occur.

The next day we shared by written word with Melena her real name. She got excited and wrote down that only special people knew this and that it was her secret, having never told anyone. She opened up to us saying she knew all the healing plants on the island and had been learning from the fairies and elves for seven years. She had total contact with Devic forms and was also telepathic. She wrote down the fairy alphabet for us and proceeded to explain some of the events the fairies participated in, in her garden. I was recovering from a sprain on my right ankle (the broken one) and she offered to help heal it. Melena and her sister performed an hour ceremony under the stars on the full moon. She covered parts of my body with mud as we sat on the earth. Her actions were very conscious and I felt honored by her presence.

Melena is a very special being, who is too sensitive for much of human conditioning. She asked us why people had so many bad thoughts - she could clearly read people's minds. I told her they had lost contact with their Inner Light and had forgotten they were Divine Spirit. I said for her not to worry for people, rather to stay happy - for her light was healing for others just by being around her. Melena is in touch with an added dimension of her existence. She is close to her Divinity, and will, I pray, awaken her full Christing in the near future by incarnating fully into the earth. This is also a timing ordained by the "Mother."

A Christed being is a very sensitive being who can not tolerate gross surroundings. To become Christed we must be willing to take on the journey to become all of who we are in truth.

To live this truth, and know we are free, is to know that we have come to participate in the co-creation of a new humanity. We of the Oneness will collectively be the "Christ Body" or the "Body of the Khalsa (Pure of Heart). Virochana's teacher, Yogi Bhajan, said this will be birthed in the year 2011 amidst much turmoil. The integrating of the earth's new frequency is the embracing of our individual and collectively Christed Self. This is achieved by releasing all our karmic limitations.

This is where we find Kundalini Yoga to be invaluable, for it maintains the voltage of a constant upward flow of energy at times to overcome all contraction and inertia. When the energy of an enlightened experience descends, one must have the strength to deal with unreleased karmas with the assistance of One's teacher and skilful techniques. We have seen people fall back into negative emotional states, such as blame, doubt, judgement, and guilt. It takes much grit and honesty to become Self Realized, and stabilized Kundalini activation is only for those ready for Self Mastery. There are limited teachings which reinforce people's self doubt and limitations and say Kundalini Yoga is dangerous and unnecessary. We know this to be a quick and difficult path, and it is not for everyone. It is not for those who do not wish to become conscious, to wake up, to become the God light that they are, and who are not willing to die to their limitations and separative viewpoints.

All of us are subject to the time and space factor here on earth. Virochana and I realize that as we are assisting in bringing the future to earth, we have to deal with the resistance from unenlightened people. We maintain our enthusiasm and strengthening by inner stimulation, meditations in the ONENESS, and balanced outer activity. This is how we maintain a regenerative body. Your body, until fully ascended, is either degenerating or regenerating.

The awakened new humanity will live in sensitive environments with pure air, water and food, and will enjoy creative, ecstatic relationship with all of creation. This new humanity will be sensitive to the Devic kingdom, and the Mother will serve those beings. We will always be growing in Love, and our lives shall reflect this state.

The next step spiritually is to achieve the Eternal Ascended physical body. The Ascended body is ordained ultimately through the Grace of the Ascended Eternal Master MahaAvatar BabaJi who holds the doorway of that Grace on this planet, as the Maitreya. This Eternal Master has held one youthful, totally transformative body on the earth for an unknown amount of time. Some say perhaps a little over two thousand years.

BabaJi is beyond all description and is known by many names. We know Him as BabaJi, also as the incarnation of Krishna, and Padmasambhava[2] in which he displayed a different face of his same current embodiment. Padmasambhava is known as the father of Tibetan Buddhism, having arrived from India into Tibet in the eighth century. Some know him as the Maha-Avatar spoken of in Yogananda's "Autobiography of a Yogi." He is also known as the Divine Director and holds the office of the Maitreya. All this we have been shown on the inner planes.

He monitors all the comings and goings on this earth. BabaJi oversees the Kundalini Shakti of this planet. He works intimately through his extended body of the Kumaras, and through 1500 entities in whom his radiations and consciousness are eternally connected. His Love is boundless in response to all of creation.

---

[2] This was shown on the "inner" in dream transmission.

He has initiated over twenty different schools of spiritual practices throughout the centuries, and it is through His Grace along with the other Beloved ascended Masters and the Mother that we can now help bring through the teachings of the Beloved Twin Rays and the Goddess.

These teachings are a blending of some traditional, radical, and personal understandings.

After a period of nine months in Kauai we felt it was time to start teaching what we had learned. Shortly after this Virochana received a letter from (Sri) Yogi Bhajan requesting us to start a teaching Ashram in New Zealand.

Our friend Harmony suggested that before we moved out of Hawaii we give a series of introductions to this teaching in Honolulu. It was set up in an unorganized way, and we saw from the start we would need to have competent people to assist us with venues. It was a good lesson in having to bring a professional attitude to our work on the earth plane. We realized we needed to develop this skill if we were to be effective as teachers. I would like to emphasize that difficulties and tests are put before the initiate to see how they respond, and to test their ability to deal with obstacles. Our vulnerability and sensitivity needed protection from the harsh reality of untrusting, critical, hardened beings.

An initiate is one who has seen the knowingness, whereas an adept is one who has Mastered and lives the knowingness. We have learned to keep our emotions out of the picture so that Love can bring through the highest good for the greatest number of beings. There is no easy way through these times, it is one's attitude that ultimately makes the difference. We have learned to turn the other cheek to other people's lack of understanding, and there is no one way to deal with each different situation. Each person must develop their own mastery so to speak, and it is through experience alone that this ultimately becomes matured. One consistent guideline for us, is to bring as much Love as possible to each situation. Patience and compassion never goes astray and wisdom is seeing how much each soul really wants to change for growth.

We meet at times souls who are in reaction to the established religious practices in our world. We know often this has occurred from the unpleasant experiences which leave a soul in a dilemma over how to progress. True growth occurs through surrender to disciplines and to a teacher of the disciplines. This leads One to One's own I AM presence or Higher Self. Trust is needed in this venture on the part of the disciple. It is through consciously invoking the desire to grow that one is "Graced" by the appearance of a teacher. So it is not until the soul cries out for help that a teacher appears. All fear must be overcome for the ego mind to die into Love or Oneness.

At this time, with the oncoming advent of the Collective Christing, there exists a new age belief in which the adherents strongly declare they have no need of outer teachers and that they only need to feel free, to be free. This they attempt to do by attending a few healers and healing weekend workshops. This is Self deception, and although some may experience moments of happiness they cannot stabilize this consciousness until all sense of little "I" is surrendered or obliterated.

We cannot throw out the baby with the bath water. It is foolishness to use the incoming momentum as an excuse for not doing the time honored inner work.

I have found each one of my baby steps were necessary and without the strength and guidance of my teachers I would never have found my own Light, my Twin Ray, or conscious communion with the Beloved Ascended Masters.

We trust it is all a matter of Divine timing and Grace. We know there are other Masters of the Oneness in the New Form coming forth in a light hearted way, free from organizational hierarchy, which we call Old Form.

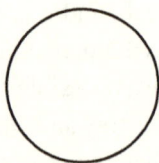

Chapter Fifteen

HONOLULU AND MORE VALUABLE LESSONS

*H*onolulu bought forth some valuable lessons. We had been very protected in many ways by the Mother in Kauai sleeping on the earth. We could not have gone through our initiations and awakenings from within the crystal grid if we did not have that total relationship with the earth. It was a demonstration of the absolute letting go of material ambition. This letting go of material ambition and complete trust was made more impactful for us at that time as we had almost no money. In fact both Virochana and I are so totally committed to the inner work and a meditative existence neither of us feel it a joy to work for money. In fact we do not even relate to the consciousness of "work." I see "work" as something people do when they are not doing what their highest joy is in that moment. Now I realize in today's climate people are fixated, hypnotized, and bound by monetary matters - yet for me I could never understand it as the source of power. I see the nine to five syndrome as a heavy karmic trap and give thanks daily for the freedom we have given ourselves, and the Grace that has come through that freedom!!!

Being without money has never meant being in poverty consciousness to me - for the Divine has always given me just enough for my needs. Monasteries and Ashrams are structures which support this letting go - and serve Monks and Nuns by taking care of their needs. It works for many - but for me I go directly to the "Mother." That does not mean it is always easy in fact I have cried, yelled and been very upset at times feeling lack of support. This has always helped to purify me more. I have had many past embodiments with great wealth and really have grown from the experience of letting my dues be paid - to balance all my karmic accounts, become more humble, and stronger in the unknown. Whatever you have to do to get stronger just do it! Its a great life and the universe always, always knows what is best for us.

One time in Kauai when we were living on food stamps, Virochana decided to start making crystal empowerment pieces for his joy of creating. I could see many different shapes wanting to come forth so he went about getting what he needed to start. He asked to borrow some tools and felt he was being blocked by one man. He began pushing the flow which is called "trying" and "struggle." I could see there was an underlying reason why these tools were not coming instantly to him. I sensed emotions that needed dealing with - some connected to his childhood and father. Virochana was not listening to me. So we went to the beach which we always did when there was any disharmony. We both lay in a stalemate on the sand. I really felt annoyed at his annoyance. After one hour he got up to go swimming and I joined him - we always do things together to work through any obstacles. Within a few minutes he was calling for help - obviously in great pain. I assisted him out of the water and he had long welt marks around his back, waist, and legs from a portuguese man-o-war that had stung him. Even though I was a few feet away I did not get stung! It was just what he needed to get in touch with his underlying emotions - such a blessing.

In a great deal of pain he asked me to drive him to a certain house where he instinctively knew there was a brother connected to this karma coming up for release. I applied aloe-vera gel to his stings and we went to the house where sure enough the brother was the only one at home. Virochana lay down and our friend and I sat with him.

He was shown what he needed to see. In the vision he saw how sixty-two hundred years ago, his present father was one of a group of eighty two beings from a star system within Orion who wanted to incarnate into the Alpha Centurion system and had been preparing themselves to this end. At that time Virochana was working in his Antarean capacity through the Alpha Centurion sun in a protective way. Virochana blocked this group from fulfilling their plans, by working within the magnetic field of the Alpha Centurion's sun. He did not feel this group energy was appropriate. This group of souls took it very hard and as a result Virochana's father and some of the others did a six thousand year sojourn on earth to work through the issues they felt with Virochana. In the process, Virochana's father prepared himself for his future incarnation in the Alpha Centurian star system. Virochana had to feel the soul pain of his father and this group. He needed to feel what it is like to be blocked and slowed down as part of the balancing of his actions. He understood the blessing to feel this pain and thus released himself and the others of the group from the need to interact again in this manner.

Virochana and I saw his father one more time in Los Angeles after we were in Honolulu. Shortly after, his father transited. He had been in great pain but grew through it. Upon leaving the body and making his ethereal completions of the earth he went to the Alpha Centurion system, where Virochana joined him in his subtle body to vouch for his father's growth and to express the Love between them.

This experience brought meaning to a dream Virochana had had several years previously in which BabaJi manifested from thin air to join him and his parents and told Virochana his father had been a great teacher in Egypt. Virochana's mother then said his father had been very afraid when she conceived Virochana - but when he saw all the inner lights and sounds he came at peace. Virochana saw how much courage this soul had by being his father and overcoming all the difficulties in this present life.

After this release on Kauai, Virochana got his jewelry tools together and began making the crystal pieces. These we sold as a sideline and still do so up until now. They have been a great joy to create.

In Honolulu we stayed in four homes over one month. After giving a talk at a downtown book shop we were invited to stay in a beautiful part of Oahu near our favorite beach there called Lani Kai.

This dear sister whom I shall call Pearl shared the home with another lady I will call Pat. This lady Pat we saw briefly on the first morning as she was leaving for work, but we never spoke. That night we went out to give another sharing, all done on donation basis. When we arrived home in Pearl's car around midnight we were locked out, and our suitcases had been put out also. We banged on the door but Pat would not let us in. She had obviously been drinking and was irrational. Pearl was staying at her boyfriend's home and we did not know how to get hold of her. Pat even called the police with a crazy story that we were dangerous. We told them we were guests, they were polite but could not help us. We had to go to a lady around the corner to ask if we could stay the night with her. She was very gracious, but very upset by Pat's behavior.

As always we did our best to remain calm and get the underlying "reason" why this was happening. We both recalled how we had been shown the emotional issues coming up for Pat on the inner planes the night before, and Virochana had also seen the police and our gear on the lawn. The lesson was that we did not act quickly enough and should have dealt with the situation immediately by talking to Pat and helping her release her fears.

Later in that day as we sat in meditation on the beach - we saw a spaceship, and Pat's father whom we understood as being on Alpha Centurion came and asked us to help her. We picked up Pearl from work and said we would like to talk with Pat. Pearl was really upset and thought maybe she would have Pat leave the flat.

Pat agreed to talk and immediately started crying. She said she had never felt so much love as she felt in us and did not know how to handle it. She had a suppressed childhood and battled constantly against her femininity. By becoming a business lady she felt worthwhile but was starting to crack at the edges. Cigarettes and alcohol were adding to her health breaking down. It was a good healing, for she began to acknowledge her more honest feelings and her own issues she needed to heal more deeply. We also did a regression with Pearl, who deeply felt that the way Pat was acting was unfair towards her, and she got in touch with some of her own issues. Through Pearl's willingness to see her limitations, she no longer needs contact lenses. She gave us the amusing title "Karma-busters."

We stayed about two weeks with them and moved on.

We are always vulnerable when travelling and staying with new people. We have learned to be more selective and have grown with experience. We need not repeat certain levels of karmic participation and now require a lot more spiritual maturity from people we move with. This is further freedom and greater Grace manifesting in our lives.

Each step must be honored and we have found there are no short cuts. From Honolulu we flew to Los Angeles to see Virochana's family for two days, and then on to New Zealand where we were given a home rent-free to stay in, and went into a three month retreat.

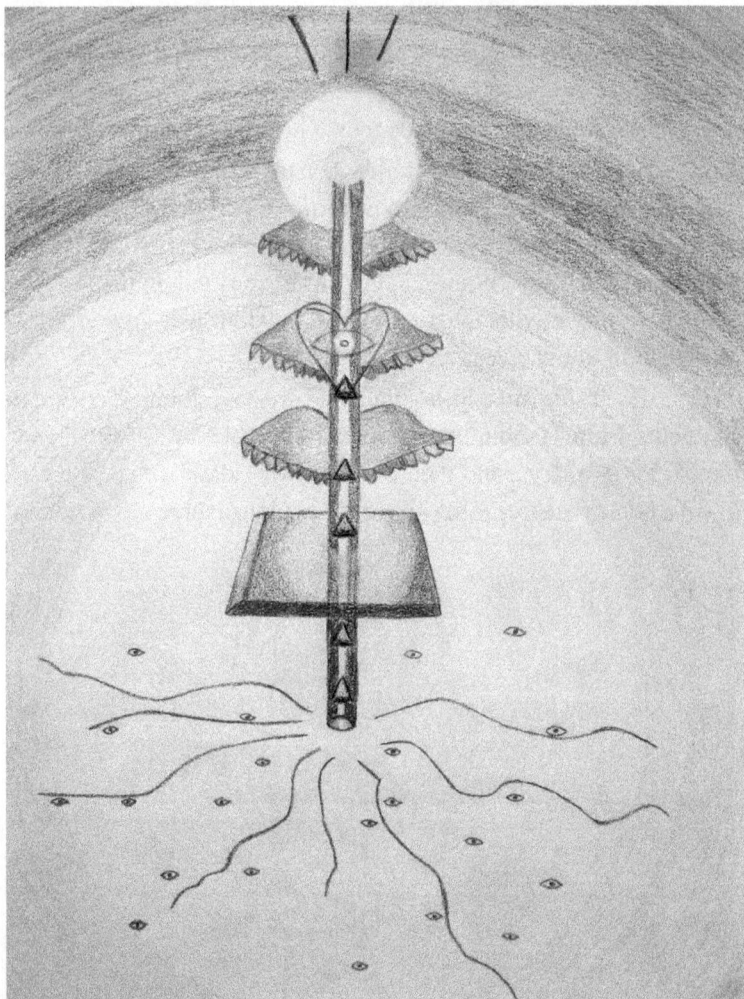

Chapter Sixteen

AWAKENING THE EARTH'S CRYSTALLINE FORM

*W*e as humanity need role models of clarity, purity, and deep insight, we need teachings that will awaken us to the realities of bliss-filled existence. We need transformative disciplines to cut through the grossness and prepare us for valuable action within the world situation.

My Beloved and I have deepened our respect for the earth as we have awoken to the reality of the earth as a living breathing creation. We have come to know the Earth as a bliss-filled conscious entity containing an emotional and etheric structure as well as physical. The etheric body is what one may term crystalline. Imagine a central point of light at the core of the earth radiating outwards towards the surface. These light beams project an interconnected gridwork upon and through the planet, forming what is called the crystal grid. They are consciously activated and resonating with the central point of light - or blueprint for the Earth's ongoing creation.

We have been shown how specific vortices within this grid carry more energy or light onto the surface of the planet, and have met beings living inside the earth on these vortices also. On the surface these vortices are experienced by people as "high energy places." These vortices are like radio stations that beam out over the planet specific thought forms which are memories within that vortex. Some of these vortices have been places of power struggles between the Light and Dark forces. Some have been, and still are, healing places to which people are drawn - feel vitalized in - and stay. As more beings become clearer and more able to collectively work for the upliftment of humanity, these healing vortices will once again have physical temples built on them. On these temple sites enlightened beings shall gather to meditate the planet more strongly into "Oneness." When the beings on the surface of earth are peace-filled, the beings within the earth will make themselves more available for growthful interchange.

One such vortex we found in New Zealand around March of 1988. Amidst our travels we decided to visit the Rotorua Lakes in the middle of the North Island. After a soak in one of the many thermal springs in the area, we looked for a suitable place to park the Van for the night. One lake stood out on the map, called Green Lake, or Lake Rotokakahi, and thus arriving at dusk, we parked by the water's edge in a secluded spot. The lake was crystal clear, and definitely had an energy about it. Countless frogs around the several mile long lake were all croaking in perfect unison in a deep harmony that was very healing to listen to, reminding one of the deep throated resonance of an assembly of Tibetan monks chanting. They would start and stop all perfectly on some inner cue.

After meditating, and getting ready to retire for the night, we both noticed out of the corner of our eyes a number of etheric beings, dressed in white, moving around in a rather unsettling way.

That night was a very active night on the inner. As revealed on the inner during sleep, the beings dressed in white were from the time of Egypt, and were known as the point teachers. Their job was to protect the Pharaohs, and to carry out clandestine operations, somewhat like our modern day CIA. They were trained in the arts of magic, astral travel, and as assassins. The point teachers, while pledging allegiance to the Pharaohs were sometimes more interested in their own agendas. An example of this was their plot to kill Tutenkarman, and a number of other persons in the court, in order to bring in a Pharaoh who was more to their liking.

The Point teachers challenged us, and we overcame them.

Then Virochana had a dream, where he found himself in a house on top of a hill about a hundred kilometers north, where we had stayed several weeks earlier. I was with him and he was motioning for me to be quiet, and that we had to move quickly. He had removed from under the floor about a dozen polished cube shaped objects, which were each like a computer storing the records of certain souls and various activities in that area. Also present was a short old lady whom I was talking to, known as the Crone, one of the many faces of the Earth Mother. I was also at this time dreaming with her, and she revealed some prophecies and details which can not be discussed at this time.

The person who owned the house in the physical was spiritually inclined, and was inwardly given that house site, to be a guardian for these cubes. The person was not fulfilling this, thus prompting the removal of the records to another site. In the dream, this person had just arrived outside the house, and in the haste so as not to be seen, Virochana dropped one of the cubes. As it hit the floor, it burst open with a brilliant almost blinding light, and vast panoramas could be seen. He picked up the cube, and we made our exit.

Virochana then went to the airport in Albuquerque, New Mexico, and in the dream the tiled floor of the airport terminal was covered in about six feet of water. He dived into the crystal clear water, bluish in color, and removed a half dozen cubes from under the tiles, similar to the ones he had taken earlier in New Zealand.

He then brought all the cubes to a small island in the center of the lake where we were camping. This island is the home of a Devic Shambhala, and in the etheric atmosphere of the dream contained many spires of light. He gave the cubes to the leader, who gratefully accepted them, and placed them in their kingdom for safe keeping. These beings helped to monitor the happenings in the local area, releasing certain memories from the earth at specific times, as the souls involved are ready. They also influence the weather in the area, as need dictates. Virochana asked the being of Light whom he gave the cubes to if he was the guardian of this place, and he looked at my Beloved and said, "no you are."

After this dream, we both had a series of dreams, where

one after the other we were shown circumstance affecting about a half dozen couples we had previously met in different areas of the world. Particularly focused around relationship, much healing was accomplished that night. We were also shown various souls who had previous incarnations as point teachers, and were presently facing these karmas.

We inwardly discovered that this area is a potential bombshell, as many unresolved violent and angry feelings have been imprinted in the ground by various souls, particularly from conflicts between the Native Maori population and the Europeans who colonized New Zealand over several hundred years. Also we later found out that a prison camp had been built on the little island at the center of the lake in the past. The Devic beings were helping to heal this, to the best of their capacity, but as always it is up to each soul involved to choose for themselves the Light.

Mountains hold a majesty about them, and are well suited as seats of power. Around Christmas 1991 we went on a three month pilgrimage to various mountains in New Zealand under the inner guidance of several Ascended Masters. Two students travelled with us, and as always adventure awaited us.

After travelling to TeAroha (The abode of Love), Mount Egmont (close connection with Mount Shasta in America), several other areas, and bringing to light some rather tricky karmas imprinted in the area of Jerusalem along a beautiful winding river with tall poplar trees, we settled for a few months near Mount Ruapehu.

Mount Ruapehu, capped year round with snow, is a majestic sight. Formed of volcanic craters, swamps, fragile desolate deserts, large lakes, and rich forests, it has a good feeling to it. Upon first arriving in the area, the four of us set up camp, then Virochana and I went for an evening walk. About an hour down the trail, at the edge of a forest, Virochana suddenly walked into the swampy forest, and hugged a huge tree. A voice was clearly heard by him, welcoming him back, saying that it had been long prophesied that he would return. It was a joyous feeling for the both of us, and the voice talked of times distant past, as if yesterday, when Virochana served from this area during Atlantean times.

For the next three nights, along the river, the Devic Lords came in dreams and revealed to him times past, and how they have affected events to the present. Mount Ruapehu is a Shambhala formed of Devic beings, many in a state of Buddhic consciousness. Some of these Devas monitor not only the earth, but other places in the Solar system as well. They showed Virochana how he had been a ruler, but that many of his court did not understand his actions, and their desires were leading them into a path of painful experience. He was well loved by the people in general, but through a plot was removed from power by those coveting it. The Devas then showed that Virochana over time started to doubt himself and withdrew somewhat. Then they showed him a meeting that would be occurring in the near future (which it did) at a retreat center near Taupo of a number of beings, all of who had fallen from grace at that time. One lady who was psychic recognized Virochana from that time in Atlantis, and she could not believe that he had come back. None of the others recognized him. (We met this lady in the physical a few months later). This knowledge was all part of a personal healing, in which Virochana could get in touch with some very profound and fundamental occurrences, thereby reclaiming the inner power necessary to stand free in the light.

The Devas referred to knowledge he held of various technologies that in the right hands can be of benefit to humankind. Also they showed him how some sought this power, ignorant of the implications of misuse. For example, a power grid made of Superconducting material would, of its own accord, radically change the subtle crystalline characteristics of rocks deep in the ground. This is possible because of certain psychoactive qualities that superconductors exhibit, not presently recognized. This would result in the stimulation of certain energies in the collective psyche and the release of past karmic scenarios at a rate too fast for many people to handle. In other words, many people would lose it, increasing the rate of breakdown in society.

The Masters, in the dream planes, showed us the ethereal connections between New Zealand, Hawaii, and the Southwest of the United States. These three areas form an extended mastery school. In the future, a human Shambhala will co-exist with the Devic Shambhala in the area of Mount Ruapehu, as it did in the distant past.

We rented a house attached to Saint Joseph's chapel in the Maori village of Little Waihi for six weeks. It was very quiet, situated along the gentle waters of Lake Taupo. Here much inner work was done. Lake Taupo, as acknowledged by many in the area holds a healing presence. Then we rented a house in a nearby village by the lake, where we held a teaching retreat and continued our meditative practices.

I am sharing these experiences as an example of some of the types of inner activity that are done regularly by beings working consciously in the Light.

Presently a number of people are tapping into these vortices. Some are healing past karmas, some are egotistically believing that they are the chosen few, and others are perpetuating recurring themes in relationships. Now is an opportune time for tremendous growth here on earth, as the crystal grid is reactivated. If you are not living your highest dream yet - it is time to eliminate all limitations including fear, doubt, and judgement, and awaken fully to play in the light which is engulfing our Earth.

The crystal grid was shut down during the sinking of the continent of Atlantis and Lemuria. This action meant that many advanced natural abilities were no longer available, as the light was withdrawn deeper into the planet. The culture of crystal technology was lost to most beings. A few spiritually matured souls maintained the knowledge, took it to Egypt, and shared this knowledge in secretive mystery schools.

Most of this crystal knowledge was reprogrammed at that time into the deeper etheric layers within the earth far beyond the conscious abilities of most beings. Some felt powerless and resentful. This was done to allow incarnate souls more time and experience in the physical, to mature in the understanding and evolutionary timing of the nature of this Earth. When humankind as a race has matured to the degree that the Mother requires, we shall see the advancement of wondrous light crystal technology. Nothing happens before its timing and we must all earn the joy and Grace that comes from spiritually maturing, and the true understanding of what it means to be Love God/Goddess embodied on this earthly paradise. Mankind then will learn from and co-create with the Devic forms that hold this planet together. Our present polluted cities have been created because humankind does not yet Love themselves, nor the earth. These pollutants are an outer reflection of people's inner turmoil. Thoughts become things when dressed by feeling. We must purify and elevate our emotions or feeling nature to bring harmonious, beauty-filled manifestation.

Humankind currently faces an enormous potential for growth or destruction. False economies, a false sense of security, false values, and a deluded sense of domination over the forces of nature, must give way to an incoming enlightened group of beings bringing forth Love. There is much unseen work going on by the seen and unseen Masters who are attempting to divert an increasingly inevitable series of (man made) disasters.

As my Beloved and I slept on the earth, listened to the Mother, and expanded in "Love," we came to witness the most powerful healing force coming from "Love." This Light of Love of our bodies shines in every cell, and as we become more and more this Light, we understand earth as our abode of gentle harmonious expression.

The body was never designed to be abused and denied Love. It is Love incarnate, designed as a temple of the God force, and it is only through denial of our God/Goddess Self that dis-ease occurs.

We alone create our bodies as a place of dis-ease, or a temple of radiant regeneration, eventually becoming eternal. Through lack of alignment to this Love Light, disharmonious feelings, thoughts, and disease arises. In this state the unloved body becomes as a machine in the struggle to survive, and people seek synthetic drugs as cures.

When I see most people's bodies, I see and feel the pain of their struggle. Men who push their bodies to survive in a no-win system, becoming gross, and dying prematurely. Women also in the struggle who desensitize their body with stimulants - antidepressants - contraception drugs - and emotional eating - creating either bullemia or anorexia, and stress. Or having cosmetic surgery, forgetting true lasting beauty comes from within.

The teachings of the Goddess are the teachings which bring the power back to the body temple and to the earth. They are for those people who are willing to realign the body temple into its sensitive regenerative nature, by surrendering to the natural things on this earth and to the Light within. These teachings assist people to experience a sense of ease in their body, and true spiritual development can only occur gracefully when carried out in refined natural environments.

I have personally attained such a level of vibrational refinement that it has become totally unsatisfactory for me to place my body in dense gross vibrations as found in earth's cities. My body does not feel as alive or able to breathe light. My body is also a vehicle of transmutation, as there is no resistance to the higher frequency. When in a city, my body is at times overwhelmed by the amount of transmutation that is needed because of disharmonious activities. It is the same for Virochana, who emulates the empowered feminine principle within the male form. This is a reason (or "factor in") why we no longer stay in cities. It is necessary for each soul to recognize at some point that they need sensitive environments to release, heal, and transmute their individual denseness. Living in a city is a karma we have freed ourselves from. It takes years of spiritual purification to realign the body to its divinity and clear it of the grosser vibrations such as the need to eat more then the body needs, and to cleanse oneself of the grosser emotions such as possessiveness, anger, jealousy, greed, judgement, and lust.

AWAKENING INSIDE THE BODY IS AWAKENING THE EARTH'S CRYSTALLINE BLUEPRINT. PLEASE UNDERSTAND THAT YOUR RELATIONSHIP TO YOUR BODY AND TO THE EARTH ARE ONE AND THE SAME RELATIONSHIP. As we awaken the etheric light in the body, we are awakening our etheric blueprint contained within the earth's crystals. By becoming once again able to source our strength and joy from the inner light, we eliminate all the contraction that is felt as pain in the body. This pain is often disempowering negative thought forms and energies which we have allowed into our auric field to minimize our feelings of Self empowerment and Self worth. As I released this pain I have at times had to crawl on my hands and knees, as my back collapsed under the impact of this release. My Beloved has also removed about twelve major psychic implants that were in my astral/auric/emotional body. These were there because I had allowed certain energies into my experience that had some investment in domination of me. These energies came through people who draw on the "light" of others. The feminine by her naturally emotionally receptive nature, is vulnerable.

In our present culture there is still a tendency to point the finger "out there" as the "cause" of our problems, and many still believe that taking on some righteous cause or "doing" good is enough to change things. It is not enough to create real change. This continues the cycle of a disempowered stance, for it puts the "Power" outside each ONE of us.

Truly only a revolution of "SELF" Awakening, Loving, and Serving the Light will reveal the new humanity, who have done the "inner work," and have attained the internal voltage and purity needed to effect change on all levels within and without. Within and Without is "ONE," not separate.

Presently there is occurring a vast polarization of the Light and Dark forces on Earth. There are those Light workers taking more self responsibility and who are commanding forth more truth, more equality, righteous redistribution of resources, a withdrawal from manufacture of nuclear armaments, and non-pollutive technologies. There are simultaneously existing those beings who do not want to see the injustices they help create, and who do not want to recognize that their lives are filled with stress and undealt with emotions. This polarization is going to continue to reveal people for what they stand for. It is not a time to sit on the fence - for you may be left behind in the void.

As the planet has had higher activations stabilized, The Light has already won. **"When you are ONE you have Won."** What a great joy!

For us living in the light means embracing the knowing-ness that we are supported by the earth, and free to Live our highest dream here on earth. Your highest dream is the one brought forth by your own God I AM presence, which also benefits others. In the higher dimensions everything is understood as the One body, and with the heart chakra wide open, one resonates with what is uplifting and healing for the "Mother" and therefore humanity. The blending and trust that exist in the higher dimensions are free of the struggle of "mine and thine," and manifestation flows with Grace and ease within the Oneness.

My dear reader, do not be of the darkness that perpetu-ates confusion, turmoil and disease. The scenario of con-tinents sinking as in Atlantis is one very possible scenario by the year 2012. Yet it need not be a part of your reality, should you awaken your Light and become the Love that you are in Truth.

May the blessings of the Ascended ONES fill you.

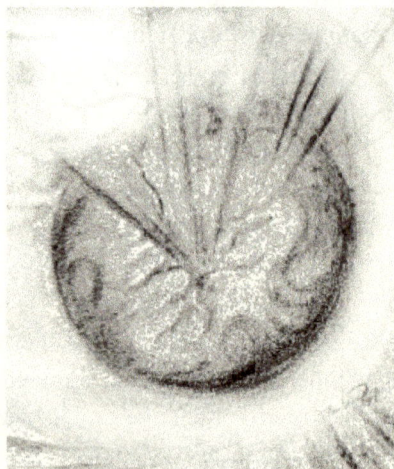

Chapter Seventeen

DECEPTIONS IN THE ASTRAL DIMENSIONS

*S*parse population, a warm climate, and cheap land have made the northern part of New Zealand a comfortable haven for alternative lifestylers.

The home we were given rent-free for ten weeks was alone on a sixty-acre property, bordered by other homesteads all on their separate blocks of land. In these areas there is much marijuana growing, and many people living on government assistance. We have found much resistance in these areas from individual and collective unwillingness to make dynamic growth. We have found when the energy of alcohol, tobacco and drugs is apparent that they represent people not wanting to take self responsibility, or even care about the need to change to a positive, healthy way of living.

Knowing this we stayed mostly to ourselves on this property. We did a strong Sadhana, and Virochana made some jewelry pieces. We got to hear about different relationship difficulties some of the neighbors were experiencing. This included physical violence and the abuse of drugs. One of the neighbors, a young woman, came to us for help. There was little we could do as her husband was not willing to let go of his drug dependency, and even though she left him for a few days under our advice, she was not strong enough to stay away from him. The emotional healing she required needed a commitment to spiritual disciplines of a strengthening, purifying nature. She felt unable to apply herself in this way, saying her two young children demanded all her time.

Over these two months we were aware of much psychic interference on the inner as a result of our being in the area. We knew it was important for our onward momentum to remain strong and clear.

Just before we were to leave the area, I had a very clear transmission one night. In this dream I was in the house with the daughter of the owners and we were chasing a demon around the house. Eventually we had it locked in the central downstairs room and I told the girl to go outside and dig a grave. She did so and I proceeded to cut up the demon into pieces that would fit in the grave. When I got to its head with fiery blazing wild eyes, it turned to me and said "Oh Shantara, if only you had sided with me, I could have given you everything!" I promptly said "That is why I could never side with you," knowing I would have sold my soul had I sided with this demon. Very lovingly I cut off its head, and we put it in the grave and covered it. Simultaneously on the inner Virochana was being shown how that land was a stronghold for old Tohunga battles. Tohungas are the Maori priesthood. This vortex had been a place where they did black magic by sending out curses and performing ceremonies before attacking other people. Virochana also dreamed with the demon who was showing him particular people who worked in various councils on this land in the time of Atlantis, and how he (the deamon) had overshadowed their workings when he could.

We understood we had been put on that land to do a strong purifying Sadhana that could break down that energy. This is one of the main reasons why there was a lot of trouble with people living in that area. It was shown to us in meditation that it was inwardly orchestrated for us to come to that area, so that we could overcome that dark force energy, and the obstructions it generated, before our next step would open up gracefully.

Our next move did happen gracefully. A very dear, wise, elderly lady came to meet us from 200 miles away. She was brought to us by a mutual friend and stayed two nights. One week later, to our surprise, we received a note from her in the mail and two bus tickets inviting us to come and stay with her. She knew we had very little money and therefore sent us the tickets. We moved on and stayed happily with our new friend for almost one month. We were then guided to be in the beautiful part of New Zealand where we had seen the golden spaceships. Though we did not have enough money to pay the rent, we rented a home which was clean, spacious, and well equipped. This we did on trust, knowing we were in the "right" place and believing we would manifest what was needed for our livelihood. As always, with much Grace we made it through, and the money came via people literally "showing up" for teachings and retreats. Here we started teaching individual and group retreats for three to five days. The crystal energy in that area is very strong and we were supported by the Mother and the Oneness in that dynamic energy field. In several dreams, the area has been referred to as "Coromandel's city of Fire" (Coromandel being the name of the peninsula we were on.)

It has become obvious to us how only certain positive vortices of the crystal energy can hold our energy. These positive vortices create for us safe havens where we feel protected by the Mother. It has become unnecessary for us to live in more dense energy fields.

The arena of our earth is a constant battle field to bring the Christ-Light of ONENESS into manifestation.

As one awakens on the inner planes one becomes truly aware of how immense this battle is, and how we have set ourselves an enormous task to awaken into the "Light." These inner planes are instructive, dangerous, unstable, and not to be joyously pursued by those souls seeking the true white Light. Limited teachers (both men and women) of certain fourth and fifth dimensional understandings have established themselves in the arenas of control on this earth. They heavily influence governments, economies, banks, and religions. They are, from a limited point of view, the most "clued up" on how to maintain control on this earth. Many of these limited masters are not totally conscious of their failings, and justify consistently their manipulative, dominating behavior. For them war is necessary, material power is seen as necessary, and aggression towards others is OK. They tend to be very individualistic, self righteous, and able to aggressively convince naive persons that their point of view is the best.

This subject could easily be the topic of a very long thesis on the downfall of Man - but it is not my intention to write such a thesis, as I much prefer to meditate upon and praise the glorious Light of Oneness and the Masters therein..

What I wish to convey is enough understanding of these energies to start you thinking about various aspects of your life.

For me to gain one such understanding on the subtleties of these energies, I was forced to look at one of my own limitations. After six months of being with Virochana I became aware of deep currents of disharmony inside me at times. These came to the surface in outbursts of short temper, and angry hurtful words towards my Beloved, and I often wanted to make him wrong in different situations. After six months of being together I was trusting enough to take a more honest look at myself, to find the source of my anger.

We were living in our van in New Zealand and had come to stay a few days with newly met acquaintances. I had become angry and realized it was because I felt I could not control Virochana, and I realized I did not yet totally trust him, and this was very painful. I meditated with Virochana and asked for a healing. That night in the dream plane I was running to different places on the earth uncovering mounds of lizards. They had been my allies over many embodiments. I gathered them together, built a large fire, and proceeded to tell them I did not need them any more. As I burned them I felt part of me being purified and released into the light. The next morning I was feeling very vulnerable, and cried as I asked forgiveness from my Beloved for being nasty at times. His Love is totally pure always, and we sat and meditated on the earth in the warm sun with the trees and birds. As we blended in Love I felt the physical release of the lizard energy as it moved (crawled) up and out the right side of my head. I saw how I had needed the wrathful force of this energy in the past to protect my feminine vulnerability at times. It was a great blessing to free myself of the unnecessary anger connected to this energy. The lizard energy was brought onto the planet to protect the feminine in its vulnerability against male domination. It serves us as long as we remain in separation. On returning home to the Oneness it must be relinquished totally along with other forces based in separation. This energy is grounded through women prone to vicious outbursts. Be wary around these women! It can also ground through certain men as an energy that sucks the feminine lifeforce in covert ways.

One world fifth dimensional Male Master who "grounds" the lizard energy into earth is the one who challenged us in a very dramatic night's ordeal, as I mentioned earlier in the book, when we were staying in the caravan upon our arrival in New Zealand.

This teacher's displays of phenomenal power are from the fifth dimension, and he impresses souls still in the grip of duality. Once a soul is in the Christos Light of Oneness, such displays hold little substance, for pure Love is understood as the greatest power.

These fifth dimensional energies have no impact in the "ONENESS," the "ONE" Light of the Christos, yet have a lot of power in the third and forth dimensions, which most of mankind is held in.

Many of humankind have become semiconscious conduits of these energies in varying ways. As people have allied themselves to these fifth dimensional powers for protection, or for psychic manipulation of some form or another, they have taken on certain tendencies that distort the highest soul expression, which is Love.

We have given these energies names, such as the cat, the lizard, the rat, the wasp, and the webs, and know from what realms many of them have been created. We have seen how certain souls through different associations have come to serve the very state they ultimately wish to be free from, because it exists in separation.

We have been challenged astrally many times by a number of so-called spiritual teachers who have these associations. It has been an exciting journey, especially as it is always revealing, and just through our Love we have found these things come up.

Love is an energy impossible to define. What we have come to recognize Love as, is the ability to feel everything as part of yourSelf, the ability to constantly expand the bliss and feel free of all tension. Love embraces all, yet holds onto nothing. Therefore Love never "has" to be right. The knowingness of ONESELF as Love means we have no enemies. There is nothing to prove. We are simply as Love, here to illuminate and unite with all other beings of Love. The qualities of this Love are peace, simpleness, joy, forgiveness, trust, and allowance. Love cannot blend with anything other than Love, its vibration is so pure and uncontaminated. For us, that means that there is much behavior on the Earth plane that we cannot be a part of.

We have found that it is only through the two of us working as One in the ONENESS on the inner planes that we can cut through the webs of illusion that exist. Often I will get part of an understanding through dream or vision, but it is not complete enough for a valuable understanding to come through. My Beloved simultaneously will be seeing from another aspect so to speak. Together we have unraveled many tricky situations, never forgetting our pure intention is the commitment to service of the ONE, which has enabled the Grace to be there.

It is necessary to see behind and beyond every mask in order to carry out enlightened service to assist souls, and to free oneself from all illusions. This is the cosmic power of the Twin Rays serving the Light. My Beloved is a Yogi of unfathomable depth. He has been told and knows that He attained Buddhahood five-thousand years ago, and need not be here. He chose to come back for me, to obtain the physically Ascended Body, and for the Earth. He is outwardly childlike, really happy and free at all times. He prefers simplicity, thus most beings do not "SEE HIM..."

Chapter Eighteen

INNER EARTH, SOLAR, AND RAINBOW BEINGS

$\mathcal{A}$s one awakens into full ascended mastery, there are constant ongoing revelations, and one realizes this path of knowingness is always unfolding more wonderful mysteries.

Virochana and I in this Leela (Divine Dance) have defined certain qualities in ourselves and others in order to gain a comprehensive overview of the ascension process, and to be used as guidelines for assisting one's understanding.

We have come to understand the differing points of strengths and weaknesses in each person we met. With absolute immaculate guidance from within the Oneness we realize the following, which I would like to share with you.

Let us begin with the understanding of what we term the "inner earth awareness" of each person.

An inner earth being is a soul committed to the collective Oneness and awakening of this planet. They are beings who intrinsically, though rarely fully consciously, understand the One light and have a strong distaste for violence, knowing if they harm others they harm a part of themselves. They are people who have kept a relationship with the Mother's energy, and who Love this planet as caretakers, and they often join, or have sympathy with, groups wanting to protect our sacred earth in some way. If not fully enlightened, they are often naive and gullible to manipulative forces (often feeling "overpowered"), as they do not like to see disharmony and darkness. Inner earth beings do not seek personal power or glorification, and often withdraw from confrontation, which is the nature of the beings we call Solar-beings. The Inner-Earth aspect of a soul is the developed feminine aspect, with its developed sense of intuition (tuition from within).

I have felt sadness seeing some of these beautiful souls remaining disempowered, often under the control of some dominating solar being.

Inner Earth beings have suffered greatly here. They have been under the powerful influences of certain Solar tendencies, including the exploitation of the earth's resources and the creation of dominating hierarchies. These hierarchies are held to maintain control over others, thus perpetuating separation. They cannot be overcome on earth until there are enough beings of Love willing and ready to look at their limitations and become personally stronger. This is the willingness to come into ones Self Mastery - which is all-powerful complete Oneness.

On the other hand, a solar being is a person who has an intrinsic connectivity to their personalized power. This personalization of their power has come from much experiencing in the play of separation, and all that that implies.

These experiences gain maturity in the realms of individual mental awareness, and require personalized Will to bring into physical manifestation.

This is the play in the mental realms on the fourth and fifth dimensions. All your thoughts occur on these levels!!

Being subtle in nature, they are resonating within different spaces in the Universe that are not physical. This is the connectivity to different planet's vibrations and different star systems.

Each planet represents some school of learning in our Universe. They do not just exist as pretty balls in the sky. Everything is created for some magnificent purpose.

Souls who have given themselves permission to explore these planetary frequencies, and who have gained the merit to do so, retaining some of the knowledge of those explorations, are what we call Solar Beings. They have a knowingness of themselves beyond the Collective status quo conditioning here on earth.

When not fully enlightened and clear as to their purpose here on earth, and the function of the blending nature of this earth, these Solar beings are out of synchronisity with the earth's needs and therefore their own growth. In this scenario, these beings are over-using their individual will rather than tapping into the collective needs. This is how Karma is perpetuated, and this struggle of individuality leads to mishaps, pain, disease, and eventual leaving of the body temple. When no more lessons and growth can be absorbed and integrated by a soul, death occurs as a way out -a rest for some time.

To move out of this polarization of being for either an inner earth or a solar being, we must go beyond the opposites into the ONENESS which is full mastery.

This journey towards our full mastery means developing what is called the rainbow body. The rainbow body has been spoken about by the Buddhist Masters, the American Indians, and the I AM teachings. Though the content of all great enlightened teachings may vary from culture to culture, the basic truth of the ONENESS remains consistent.

The acquiring of the rainbow body, or being a rainbow dancer or a rainbow being, requires quite simply the mastery of all the seven rays of life. There are actually more than seven rays, but they become more subtle and impossible to define.

These seven rays are red, orange, gold, green, blue, indigo and violet. Indigo and violet are the same for me, and I add pink as the sixth ray.

The rainbow beings are those souls who are willing to embrace the continuing collective experience, and blend it masterfully into their unique expression. They are able to apply the understanding of the Higher Tantra and continue the blending in the Oneness. In this way, one gains mastery of all the seven rays which create the Rainbow Body.

Acquiring the rainbow body is the goal of the rainbow beings. When souls have passed through preparatory and higher initiations, and have proven themselves as able to take on the teachings of the Oneness, they draw to themselves the strong attention of the Ascended Masters. The Ascended Masters then consciously guide and monitor the progress of the rainbow being very closely.

This is the stage Virochana and I find ourselves at now. We recognize ourselves as our own Masters fulfilling what our providence ordains. We feel strong standing in our own light, and can guide many brother and sisters to the "ONENESS" - to their own inner light. At the same time, we are totally blended with the Ascended Master's frequency, and require their direct radiations to achieve our rainbow body, or Ascended Body.

In the Buddhist teachings, the rainbow or Ascended body can be achieved before or at the time of death. It is our personal providence to attain the Ascended Body before age and death take over.

A rainbow being lives at the level of Oneness - beyond the struggle of individual karmas, and is able to integrate all experience on the level of Oneness, LOVE.

These people of Love/Oneness are the Ones who will gain this earth as Heaven. They are the beings who are the Collective Christ body now awakening.

A prophecy of this comes from the ascended Master El Morya, Lord of the Blue ray. He was also one of the Three Wise Men of the Bible, King Arthur of the round table, Apollo of Greece, an American Indian medicine woman, and Rishi Dush Dharam, a Himalayan Yogi. His last well-known incarnation was Guru Gobind Singh, the tenth Sikh Guru. In that life he left certain prophecies, including one he named the birthing of the Khalsa (meaning pure of heart), onto the planet. He said "960 million Khalsa there shall be." Sri Yogi Bhajan has said that this Khalsa shall be birthed in the year 2011 amidst great turmoil on the planet. This number quoted is approximately twenty percent of the earth's present population, and is the same number we have been given in certain prophecies.

Many will join their Twin Ray as they grow spiritually. We assist those who meet us to invoke this relationship into reality. By this our joy is increased, as more beings become lighter, happier, and more free, and maintain their own unique expression of the Oneness. We see many who come to us are preparing and wanting LOVE in form, which is the Twin Ray. We help them in this preparation through giving transformative practices and insightful guidance.

Chapter Nineteen

TEACHINGS OF THE TWIN RAY

*T*he teaching of the Eternal Beloved Twin Ray relationship is one of the most important understandings for all souls on the earth today. The coming together of the Twin Ray Flame is achieved after individual enlightenment is attained. The amount of Light and cosmic power focused through this embodied relationship is greater than any individual can ever project.

This Twin Ray relationship is the complete merging of the one Soul Flame which is sourced from the Central Sun, which when coming into form embodied both male and female. The uniting of this flame from the physical is the pouring forth once again of the full flame in its total God Light essence.

This reuniting with one's Beloved Twin Ray will happen eventually for all souls as they reach for the ascended eternal bodily state of full liberation. This state knows no death of the body ever again, it is undying, having transcended all conditions held within time and space.

This union with one's Twin Flame can occur either on the earth plane or on another planet, when both parts of the "ONE" have ascended beyond karmas of separation.

Virochana and I as the Beloved Twin Ray relationship are in process towards this final total ascension of the body here on earth, and need the direct assistance and grace of one of the already Ascended Masters to gain this.

We have gained so far the enlightened clear state which is ascension of the mind. This ascension of the mind means one is free of the karmas, thoughts, feelings, and actions which keep a soul bound in incompleteness, struggle, unhappiness, the illusion of separation, and away from their own unlimited boundless I AM Light.

This enlightened clear state is a great freedom, compared to the physical emotional and mental bondage experienced by most of humankind. Yet it is imperative that everyone knows that there is more to achieve from the level of personal enlightenment. From this personal enlightenment the soul can invoke the Beloved Twin Ray relationship, and complete the ultimate eternally omnipotent omnipresent ascension. The Twin Ray may or may not be on the earth. It is up to each person to understand how they have co-created the coming together and the timing with their Twin Ray.

I had never read of the twin ray, of my twin ray - yet I always knew I would meet my one-and-only. As my mother watched me go in and out of relationships she once said to me "What you are looking for does not exist" I instantly replied - "Yes it does, or I would not be here."

In this way I knew I could not fail to invoke this relationship of "perfection" into the physical. My Beloved and I were ordained from the "ONENESS" to come together on the Harmonic Convergence in August of 1987. Nothing and no one could stop this. Heaven and earth were moved to bring us together. In this understanding we can never say to anyone - "on such and such a day you will meet your twin ray," though many would like us to be able to give a guarantee. It is only known to you, when you are truly awakening that your twin ray is going to manifest, and the how is simply a knowingness that it will. The details will arrange and rearrange themselves as necessary.

As I have said - remember it is not everyone's creation or providence to be with their twin ray in the physical in their present embodiment.

We do understand however, that there will be more twin rays coming together on the planet at this present time, for it is the birthing of the Collective Christed body of the "ONE" - the time ordained for the Golden age.

It is my Beloved's and my Divinely co-created birthright to be as we are now in form, and to bring forth this teaching for those who are aligning to their twin ray completion.

As Beloveds working in the arena of spiritual teaching, we add an important missing component to spiritual teachings on earth, a blessed fulfilled component which is of great assistance in presenting a more complete teaching form. This is the expression of a Liberated, yet Divinely wedlocked committed couple, totally free of social conditions and equal in their love for each other.

We also strongly choose to remain in a simple, happy life-style which is in itself a great part of the teachings of the Beloveds. We have experienced through this, that any limiting tendencies on either of our parts become easily and immediately addressed. As we face the challenges of bringing in New Form.

IN THIS WAY WE LIVE IN AND MANIFEST THE LAW OF THE LIGHT THROUGH ALL SITUATIONS, DEPENDING ON NO OUTER ORGANIZATION OR FOLLOWING.

Through the Beloved Twin Ray relationship, people who are ready see a living demonstration of a light, happy, and free couple willing to embrace life. In this way we bring the supreme Divine awareness into conscious participation, thus breaking down people's sense of separation.

Virochana and I live simultaneously in four different dimensions and beyond. Living a multidimensional existence means that a person is willing and able to experience the Self, beyond any imposed limiting reality. Just because we have a third dimensional body, this does not mean our experience need be limited to the third dimension and trapped in third dimensional karmas of money, food, sex, and struggle. We are consciousness itself - not just a body - and this truth gives us the capacity to awaken in all aspects of conscious creation. People are made aware through our example that their day to day life can be something other than a struggle if they activate their "I AM" presence and apply spiritual law in all situations! It is essential that the passion for Divine experience first be awoken in each person wanting a light, happy and free life.

Because all of us concurrently exist with potential to awaken forth and fifth dimensional reality, forth and fifth dimensional beings are aware and communicating with those of us in the third dimension whom are awake enough, if and when we choose to communicate. We have come to understand why on the forth and fifth dimensions there are differing levels of evolved and not-so-evolved beings. A person with a third dimensional body capable of extending their consciousness beyond the fifth dimension and beyond the light to the "ONE" is a teacher for many forth and fifth dimensional bodied souls. If you can grasp this truth you can have many wonder-filled revelations.

ASCENDED MASTERS WORK IN ALL REALMS OF EXISTENCE ON MANY PLANETS, THROUGHOUT MANY SOLAR SYSTEMS.

In the arena of spiritual enlightenment, I also experience the reality of women needing to be given equal recognition. In every arena on the earth this drive towards equality for women is gaining more and more attention, but we as a humanity are making slow progress. It is more difficult for people to accept a woman's enlightenment than a man's. There are traditional Hindu teachings which state that a woman must be reborn as a man to achieve liberation. This is not true, I have proven it myself.

There is also a great deception for some people in that they want to see enlightened people as able to produce outer phenomena, and my Beloved and I do not fit into this expectation, and never will. One well-known teacher whom we have had hundreds of interactions with on the inner, and who calls himself The World Saviour, has come to me and offered me all his siddhis (powers). I lovingly replied, "Thank you, but I have all the powers, ..." My reply surprised me for outwardly I do not even think about power, other than the recognition of the power of Love - Oneness. This teacher outwardly displays his magnetic charisma and subtly hypnotizes his devotees. A karma which He will free himself from one day, as he wakes up! As mentioned elsewhere in the book, living the Divine Self is the greatest miracle of all, and to simply be, and allow the Divine Leela to dance through One's form, is all the miracle one will ever require. Inner phenomena occur every time you meet a teacher or teaching on the inner.

Therefore we do not seek any spiritual powers called siddhis. Yet we know and watch how the Divine law works perfectly at all times. A conscious pure being is exposed to all the shamanistic realms, and when becoming a teacher one needs to be a great warrior to protect and defend at times. We have had a lot of experiences in this arena. Our highest expression is simplicity, stillness, and Love of pure being. Our passion to remain clear is paramount.

Our ongoing commitment to greater unending expansion is a teaching in itself, what we call an inclusive teaching. It is a bringing forth of Divine eternal truths and applying the unbreakable laws of life. Out of the obeyance and demonstration of these laws, a world of perfect harmony can be created for everyone.

This teaching is in direct opposition to so many existing spiritual teachings which are exclusive. In other words, the teachers of these exclusive teachings are unwilling to integrate new methods and greater Divine qualities, which a growing organic dissemination of Divine laws should do. One of these old-form exclusive teachings is the tendency to want escape from the body.

This teaching gives prescribed forms of meditation that do not address bodily emotional issues. This school of thought propounds the idea that meditation is about experiencing life on the inner planes, called astral or etheric experiences, and a good deal of the focus of these teachings is to bring about this awakening in people.

Practitioners over a period of years, or even lifetimes, perform prescribed meditative techniques that open the inner vision, by focusing their attention on the form of their teacher within the third eye point. This practice specifies not to bring One's awareness below the sixth chakra. One becomes gradually aware of the inner sight, and thus wakes up to astral travelling and inner revelations, but this can take lifetimes to perfect. Meditating on the "light" of someone else rather than one's own inner life is another way to give power away. One will never achieve full Self Mastery in this limited experience. We have found the tendency for people involved in these practises to put an insufficient and unbalanced amount of attention and energy into their enjoyment of relationships, their bodies, and the love of being here on earth. These techniques do not include conscious physical techniques to purify, realign, and strengthen the physical and emotional bodies that bring ecstasy into every organ and cell.

This negation of the body is also negation of the earth, and many karmas of fears and doubts are never transmuted in many of the practitioners. This school of thought declares the earth as a very dense realm of existence, and One needs to get out of it as quickly as possible to discover heaven elsewhere. It also propounds that the body is "just a vehicle" to carry out earthly obligations. This thought minimizes one's ability to experience the physical body as "Bliss itself."

The body for us *is the Soul* expressed in form - It is not separate from the soul. When you *feel* your body as your soul, you are on the right track to Self Mastery in every dimension of form.

However in the escapist mind set, it is never possible to experience Liberation ecstatically here on earth. Additionally, the limited teachers in these teachings are worshipped as being the Light itself, and they claim that they alone are able to set the students free. By allowing this, people are still denying their own inner Light, and see the inner Light as the Master. Separation of their own soul is thus perpetuated. Another limitation of this mind set is that it does not acknowledge the power of the Mother, or allow the total surrender (trust) and alignment to the Divine Mother.

After many spiritual experiences, one will eventually realize this earth as the Great Mother's body of bliss, and be totally at ease with manifest existence, thus becoming Liberated.

Whatever we resist persists. This is a great truth, and we as Beloveds have Realized there is nowhere to go: rather it is a question of bringing all of who we are, Love, Truth, Bliss, into every part of the body to transform matter into the daily joy and lightness of being. We call this the descension process rather than escapism. In this way we are able to co-create heaven on earth.

Life was never meant to be a hardship. It is rather the very highest expression of Love to incarnate in third dimensional existence and have the grand opportunity to awaken the Self from the infinite down into the finite earth. Here we can play as God/Goddess in form, which when awoken, is bliss itself.

Change is growth, and the greater the change often the greater the growth. Therefore, as an evolving humanity we must always be willing to reconstruct old understandings into greater truths, or we remain static. As long as we believe that we have all the answers we remain static.

This is a great truth, and Virochana and I have on a number of occasions put ourselves out to meet and co-create with other teachers. We consistently find there is no room for us, and that these beings are enjoying life as a big fish in a small pond, as opposed to being a small fish in the unlimited ocean of Oneness. We understand this will soon change for some.

This has shown us the reality that we must forge ahead

slowly in our teaching with those that come to us. Our position is to encourage and assist in bringing forth the unique master filled expression of each person. We teach therefore in a framework which does not pride itself on boundaries.

It is a teaching that I call a finishing school, rather than a teaching that perpetuates dependence on something outside of One. We are assisting in preparing the initiates into Christ consciousness - what an incredible joy.

Often on the planet we have witnessed how people end up serving a religion or political system, and how the individual expression is sacrificed and manipulated for that religion or system.

Now is the time on earth where in every arena humankind is being forced to acknowledge what is no longer of value or acceptable to people and our earth. As the cleansing of ourselves and the earth continues over the next twenty years, there will be no rock left unturned. Each and every person will easily see their self-created heaven or hell. Each person who awakens their own "light" will understand their body as an extension of the earth.

We can no longer look to things outside us or the planet to save us. The answers are now, and always have been, within us. The coming into our Christ Light, our Christed Selves, will bring into form greater numbers of the twin ray relationship than ever before experienced on earth.

The LOVE of this outpouring is the healing we all need. The twin-ray teaching represents the healing of ourselves and all personal relationships, including our relationship with Mother Earth.

Chapter Twenty

CELIBACY, SEXUALITY, AND THE BELOVEDS

*C*elibacy is a state of being that requires deeper understanding by most people. Along with sexuality and Love, it has been the tool of much distortion, and manipulated states of being. I have come to see two very different ways that people enter into celibacy.

The first way is a way which I neither agree with nor would advise for any person wanting total awakening empowerment and enlightenment. This I call the celibacy of suppression. It is an old limited way, in which people think that if they just suppress and deny their emotions and feelings, they will conquer their God-given energy of dynamic interaction. Having seen intimately a number of men in this state, I can say quite clearly that this denial is like building a dam that is never going to be big enough to hold all the water that is being backed up. At some point in time the walls will crumble, and the flood of emotions and feelings must be acknowledged. It may be some kind of balancing the scales for misuse of sexuality in the past or a form of punishment, yet it is only a partial remedy.

A total cure for the misuse and misunderstanding of the sexual energy is to completely understand it - and transcend it in a natural grace-filled and pure way.

The second way of celibacy is what we call "true celibacy." IT IS THE STABILIZED UPWARD FLOW OF ENERGY IN THE BODY TEMPLE, WHICH TRANSMUTES ALL GROSS EXPRESSION.

Personally my sexual expression was always that of a Tantrika (one who has overcome lust and knows the body energies and functions as all Divine). I never had difficulty expressing my Love in a sexual relationship with men whom I chose. I have never qualified my energy as sexual, and never understood how people could. This understanding is a basic essential requirement for one wanting to practice Tantra. This inherent knowledge was always natural and freeing for me as I could explore all my inner emotions and get rid of what I did not want. This was a yogic skill I had mastered in my previous embodiment, bringing it forth consciously from birth.

To assist one involved in intimate relationship, an understanding of what Red or sexual Tantra is will be helpful. Red Tantra first needs the mastery of the upward flow of energy in the body. It then needs a foundation of purity and wholesome connectedness within the body. Once these two schools are established, all necessary understandings come through appropriate relationship.

Traditionally Red Tantra is contained within the path of "Vajrayana" which means "indestructible path." Tantra is recognized as a fast and dangerous path to enlightenment, as it is a teaching which encompasses all experience as a means of growth and denies nothing. It is a strengthening passion for ongoing Divine Intimacy, and a practitioner must have this passion. If this is not established, a red tantra practitioner will fall into the muck of emotions and become enmeshed in karmic entanglements. Many advanced Yogis fall in this way. The lower sexual nature means a weakening and expulsion of energy.

RED TANTRA IS SUCCESSFUL ONLY FOR THE MOST MATURE SPIRITUAL PRACTITIONERS, WHO PRACTICE ENERGY CONTROL, HAVE A STRONG UPWARD FLOW OF LIFEFORCE, AND CAN CIRCULATE SEED ESSENCE. Red Tantra can only be practised, successfully and gracefully, by people who have freed themselves from all emotional dependency. Allowing with deep respect the absolute freedom of one's partner is paramount.

True celibacy arises naturally when all seven chakras are activated and One experiences the inner joy of opening the inner spaces. The eighth chakra must be opened also which allows this upward transmutative flow to be strong, and the Arcline to be strong. (The Arcline is the halo-like band of light depicted around the head in paintings of some saints.)

This naturally-occurring celibacy is not a neurotic suppression of the second chakra, where lustful thoughts still play.

True celibacy is a state of being when there is no need to release pent-up tension through the second chakra. When blending sexually from an enlightened state, the bliss is experienced in every cell of the body, and the internal elixirs regenerate One's whole being. Thus One's attention is free, and this is what we call a celibate state.

We believe that this complete blending is only possible with the "Beloved Twin Ray," as there are no unfinished karmas to be dealt with now or in the future. The attempt to make a sexual relationship into something "perfect" which it is not destined to be, is to create struggle. People may stay in one marital relationship for a whole lifetime, completing some karmic pattern. Yet now is the time on earth when more people are experiencing the need to free themselves quickly. People's movements through sexual relationships of a karmic nature are being completed and released more speedily. This is absolutely essential for your attainment of liberation. It is vital that as a humanity, we learn to free ourselves and others more quickly: emotionally, and on all levels. This is being activated by the incoming higher planetary frequency. When a soul is spiritually ready for SELF MASTERY, the awareness of the already created Beloved Twin Ray relationship will come to them if they have set it up that way.

Until One is with the Beloved Twin Ray, in form there will always be a degree of dissatisfaction in relationships of a sexual nature. Do not judge yourself because you cannot make a relationship work. Take the learning and be free.

After blending fully with my Beloved Twin Ray, the state of celibacy automatically arose for me at the age of forty, and in absolutely no way is denial a part of this natural state of being. We enjoy a full intimate expressive LOVE which requires minimum genital contact. This state is impossible to describe as one must experience this fulfilled Oneness with their Twin Ray to understand fully.

In the natural course of time as one matures in this Beloved relationship, and spiritual maturity becomes a daily reality, sexuality becomes less in focus. There is in this state a stabilized pure awareness, which is living in the Oneness at all times. This opening of the higher centers increases the lifeforce in the body, and the naturally arising bliss and ease creates total harmony in every moment.

As the "ONENESS" becomes a more complete reality, even the need or the desire to blend sexually does not arise. We have come to understand pure sexuality (not the perverted manipulation of another's lifeforce which happens) as the desire (need) to blend in the Oneness. When everything (thought, action, word) is blended with the Beloved Consciousness, One is complete, and working in the Higher Tantras. Here we stand in total obedience and harmony with the Law of the One.

Intimate Relationship of a Loving eternal nature comes out of Self Mastery. **IT IS TRUE WE CAN ONLY LOVE ANOTHER TO THE DEGREE THAT WE HAVE REALIZED OUR "ONE" ETERNAL SELF, AND LOVE THAT SELF.** Love arises as we awaken our Self into the "Oneness" and proclaim our light as the 'ONE' with the Christos light, which illumines all darkness and casts out all fear that comes from the illusion of separation.

We understand the Beloved Relationship has happened for us, as we have committed our life to the "ONENESS." This commitment on both our parts set the stage for us to meet. We see how true lasting happiness is found through awakening Self Mastery, giving out and receiving Loving thoughts and actions, and dedicating one's life to serving the light in all beings.

In the arena of relationships, people's troubles, suffering and disharmony in their intimate relationships are directly as a result of being off track spiritually. As mentioned earlier, it is true that until a person has achieved enlightenment in the ONENESS, all relationships are karmic - a ground for completion of a certain emotional experience and growth for each soul. It is a shame to see how many couples bind each other both sexually and emotionally, thereby remaining in dependency addictions. The experience of limitation carries on for lifetimes in numerous ways, until the Beloved Self is reunited with, and obeyed totally.

The righteous, undeniable, unavoidable, unseen law of Love and Oneness is at work every moment in every soul's existence. It is up to each individual to look within, listen to the inner Ascended Masters, and fulfil this law. With spiritual fulfillment comes knowledge, abundance, happiness, Love, and peace; for all receive equally exactly what is due to them as a direct result of their thoughts, intentions, actions, sanskaras, and providence.

This is our experience, and upon meeting we knew we could never part, for we were already One on every level. This is a profound realization, and not to be diluted in any way. One is ready to meet their Beloved Twin Ray after they have completed all karmic relationship.

Once established in the Twin Ray relationship, which is the marriage co-created in heaven, one is initiated into the higher tantric mysteries , i.e., awakening the "mysteries" into mastery. All emotional and mental healing occurs naturally early on in the Beloved relationship, and lovemaking is a natural expression to regenerate, bond, and be ONE. The couple must continue to maintain a disciplined Self Responsible and uplifting life. One's Divine powers are awoken quickly in this Love, and One gains natural awareness to master all gross expressions through energy control. This is a teaching very greatly needed by humanity.

Now is the time that more souls ready for Liberation are incarnating. They have already set it up to be free, unite with their Beloved consciousness, and meet their Beloved Twin Ray here on earth in order to manifest the living forms of this Beloved relationship. It is up to the providence of each Beloved couple how they will take the red tantric path.

These Beloved couples will bring through the new root race, the children they have will be very advanced souls. We as humanity need role models in enlightened Loving relationships. This is what is required to co-create a new harmonious society, and will bring peace on a larger scale.

To Be One with Another, One must First Be One With the True Self. This is Self Love, Self Awareness, Self Realization.

UNIVERSAL LOVE AFFAIR

The Beloved relationship is the microcosm in the macrocosm. This is the true state of the whole universe, which is One great Love affair.

Everything we perceive and do not perceive that is in existence is created out of LOVE ONENESS. As we open more to who we are, which is Love, that is all we can experience.

Every leaf, every sound, every cell of creation is of the same stuff - LOVE BLISS.

We exist in it because of it. There is nowhere out of this state, and all we can do is to gradually lift our vibration into this state of total TANTRA.

There is nothing that can be added to this, it is "The Light," all encompassing, vibrating, complete and free of any contraction.

This is all we are here to realize. This is the gift we gave to ourSelf. One, as One, with all of that which is.

Rejoice, Embrace life, be Free, do what ever it takes to remain in ecstasy.

My Beloved and I created the Beloved relationship to be in at all times. We bring this gift to earth to share with beings who choose the Oneness, and who will also be in Beloved relationship.

Out of this is the ongoing experience of completion and Christing, liberation, and happiness.

Out of this all is healed and fulfilled.

Out of this the God/ Goddess is awakened into Divine Leela.

The Universal Love Affair awaits your participation...

Chapter Twenty One

TECHNIQUES TO ELEVATE AWARENESS

Discovering and Revealing The True Nature Of SELF..

It is beyond form, therefore it is not contained within personality.

It is beyond duality, therefore it is beyond mind.

It is beyond the light, therefore dependent on nothing.

It is all encompassing, therefore not limited in its location.

We become One with it, yet cannot own it.

We become One with it by relinquishing personality, mind and attachment to form.

A being may be enlightened as to the true nature of existence, yet there are stages. Even Liberation is both a static and fluid state, there is always more, for the Oneness is unlimited.

We, as consciousness reviewing and revealing ItSelf to the Self, are the greatest miracle of all. Therefore, why bother to seek miracles, or proof of power? By being consciously ordinary, One can hold in truth all that is extraordinary. For it is just integrating more of that which we already are...Self.

AFFIRMATIONS

To reach your goal spiritually, you must believe whole heartedly that it is possible. This requires a positive, definite attitude of mind. The words we use in every sentence emit a vibration which subtly shapes an auric resonance around us.

The sound or tone of our voice and how we speak gives a total picture of how we perceive ourselves inwardly, and therefore how the Universe perceives us. To change our energy from a downward flat, negative vibration, to an upward, vibrant positive one, means saying and speaking in a positive tone.

This is where affirmations are essential to assist one's cleansing of the mental body especially, but also it impacts and brings about healing needed in the emotions. These positive affirmations cannot be overlooked, and I consider them an integral part of a total healing and elevation of one's spiritual process.

Take a look at some of the affirmations below as examples of what may help you. You will notice they are qualified by the "I AM." When one uses "I AM" they are automatically setting into action their Higher Self - aligned with the omnipotent ONENESS - and all the Ascended Masters' collective resonance of that same "I AM" frequency. Your "I AM" is beyond any limitation of personality, and brings direct contact with your soul.

**I AM the Soul
I AM the Light Divine
I AM Will
I AM Love
I AM Fixed Design**

I AM the perfection of all relationships.

I AM the presence removing all obstacles surrounding me.

I AM the Light of God that never fails.

I AM the Clarity of total understanding of all I need to know.

I AM the forgiveness of all unenlightened deeds.

I AM the presence bringing forth radiant youthfulness into this body temple.

I AM the illumined mind radiating in the hearts of all God's children.

I AM the only presence here.

I AM here I AM there I AM everywhere doing what needs to be done.

As you see, each of these affirmations deal with some issue pertaining to your everyday existence. Some are directly handed down from the Ascended Masters - mostly Saint Germain - through the I AM teachings. Some are what we have bought forth and use daily.

No one owns the "I AM" presence: give yourself licence and bring forth your own affirmations as required. They have the power to help change your life if you use your full love and intention, but you must be consistent. Do not give up after a few weeks because there is no great miracle, apply yourself daily for at least one year. This is the inner work - you will need to address all the areas in your life that are suppressing you spiritually.

KUNDALINI YOGA

This yoga has been called the Yoga of awareness. It includes aspects of other Yogas such as Hatha, Raja, Kriya, Nada, Laya, Tantra, Martial arts, and Shamanistic understandings. I have found it to be extremely beneficial in providing a time- honored complete platform on which to develop spiritual mastery.

It is necessary to learn Kundalini Yoga from a competent teacher as there is much acquired skill which must be transmitted through the teacher. Virochana is such a teacher, and it was through the strength and Grace of His teacher, Sri Yogi Bhajan - who brought this form to America in 1969, that it can now be taught. An experienced teacher is also necessary to assist a practitioner through the stages of the awakening of the Kundalini power, which at times is so dramatic that the teacher's clarity and inner transmissions are invaluable.

Kundalini Yoga is a balanced application, dynamically strengthening the body with movement, breath, sound, and Kriyas. It is a very effective practice to cut through neurosis of the mind, to release contracted emotional blockages, free agitation of the body, and to prepare a person for silent meditative Sadhana. Although I had practised other yogic disciplines, Kundalini yoga was necessary to bring me more strongly into my body, and it continues to benefit me as I apply it almost daily. A person develops strong roots when applying it, and we consider it one of the essential techniques.

As a science, Kundalini Yoga is very practical. It starts with purifying and penetrating exercises of body, mind, and emotions. Until you reach a certain level of purity, it is hard to feel the purity within you. It is the feeling of that purity which awakens the feeling of your blissful Divinity. It is the power of penetration into the cellular memory which brings up all limited experience. These are all worked through with the tools of Kundalini Yoga.

Kundalini Yoga opens all the chakras, and brings up karmic cellular memory for releasing quicker than other yogas. I have found it to be the difference of travelling ten miles-per-hour in one's evolution in other yogas to travelling one hundred miles-per-hour in one's evolution doing Kundalini Yoga. It opens the inner spaces very quickly, and gets us in touch with the deeper currents of our being.

Along with the Kriyas, the dynamic movements of Kundalini Yoga are in my experience, an invaluable practice for every person who is wishing to grow spiritually, and is in average health. The Kundalini is the vitality coiled at the base of the spine awaiting its conscious awakening and complete opening. Awakening the Kundalini is an essential first step for a person intending to create an eternal physical body.

STANDING MEDITATIONS

These are fundamental martial arts techniques - specifically, internal style techniques. These martial arts stances and Chi Gung, which was originally a Chinese meditation form accentuating breath techniques, are very valuable for developing internally strong equilibrium, thus healing and strengthening the organs of the body.

These techniques help align the skeletal system, cleanse toxins and fears from the joints, tendons, muscles, blood, and cleanse the bones themselves.

Standing meditation includes pranayama, visualization, control of mind, and is invaluable for developing a regenerating body. Many of these methods have been kept in "secret" schools with long, slow, arduous training for years. It is only in the past ten to twenty years that much of this knowledge has been made freely available - because mankind needs it and is ready. These standing meditations help prepare the physical vehicle to hold the voltage of pure light as the chakras are opened and karmic cellular memory is released. They are in our experience one of the most valuable, effective, and "skilful means" that we have to cleanse, strengthen, and elevate our bodies and emotions.

HONEST EXPRESSION

We encourage our student practitioners to examine every area of their life, to discover if what they are doing is a truly fulfilling expression of who they are. This usually requires that they are faced with great changes as they realize how they have limited their truthful expression in many ways. The practice of empowering oneself to live One's truth takes courage and constant willingness to move forwards, to trust, and to expand. There are no limitations except the ones we put upon ourSelf, and to work only for money crushes the lifeforce of a soul. Working primarily for a pay check is a common third dimensional karma.

To become truly free, One must have an honest livelihood which reflects your highest joy possible in present time. To do this, all limitations must be overcome, such as fear that the Universe is not totally supportive. This may include overcoming the consciousness of greed which is always fear based. Living an honest expression is the only way each of us will eventually rise out of the swamp of illusions.

PREPARATION FOR THE BELOVED RELATIONSHIP

One of the greatest joys we have is sharing the Love we experience as Beloveds. This immediately brings into close focus the people around us, and how they are functioning with their intimate relations. We have found that couples either go through dramatic reawakening of the Love between them and of the reasons they are together, or they separate very quickly, when coming into our orbit and reflection[1]. We see a major part of our service as assisting in preparing people for the Beloved relationship. This means first developing a strong Loving relationship with one's Self, clearing away all feelings of lack of Self worth etc. Love knows no fear or doubt, and through clearing away all restrictive innate tendencies of Self contraction, a practitioner gains true Loving Self-awareness.

From this level of growth, a person is then able to invoke and attract into their life at the right timing their already created Twin Ray. Living with the Twin Ray is "living on a Karma-free diet." We understand the great depths of intricacies involved in this preparation, and each person's process is therefore unique. Each of us needs wise inner dialogue and patience in taking the steps towards the Twin Ray, and must be willing to do whatever it takes to gain this lofty fulfillment.

---

[1] By seeing their intimate relationship as a block to further spiritual growth.

FAMILY RELATIONSHIPS

Extending spiritual disciplines to children is absolutely essential in developing a harmonious household. Children are naturally meditative, and can be included in family meditations daily in a wise and gentle way.

By creating a meditative harmonious atmosphere children respond positively. This means the parents are involved in daily disciplines which can be made enjoyable for children to share. Naturally one does not expect a child to sit in silent Sadhana for hours on end. Only exceptional souls will express the desire for this practice. Even if a child does not sit silently, they can be engaged in creative visualization and meditative relaxation techniques. Generally speaking, children from around four years can do and enjoy gentle Yogic postures and easy breathing techniques.

By consciously returning a child to themselves, they are able to maintain a strongly connected identity with life. They must feel their strength and happiness as a child in order to feel the strength of connectivity to all life. Children respond very quickly to the energy around them, be it positive or negative. I have noticed often how children will dramatize an underlying energy of their parents which is not being addressed. They also play out the violence of television and movies. This is a terrible way to influence the pure mind of a child. In other words, we will have happy children consistently when we have happy parents, harmonious natural environments, and schools that encourage balanced loving Self awareness, and greater Self understanding through teaching and acknowledging applied spiritual principles.

Parents are chosen by the incoming soul to give them the greatest opportunity for completing karmas and growth. As a child matures, they become all too aware that their parents are not en-lightened. At this point children start to draw away from the parent's influence, to bring forth more of their own Self expression. This is often uncomfortable and confusing for the young adult. If there are negative attitudes and lack of communication from the parents, this adds to the confusing thoughts and unexpressed emotions of all parties. This perpetuates the feelings of painful separation. The only way out of this is for people to constantly be willing to grow, to be totally honest, and to be willing to purify their contracted negative tendencies and communicate from a heart feeling.

All parents need to be set free from the limited role as parent, and it is usually only when a child experiences their self freedom that this is possible. Setting our parents free with Love is a great step forward into spiritual maturity. It is the generation that I belong to now that has probably initiated this event to a far greater degree than ever before. By using the words "setting free" I am not implying that we should abandon our parents when they need us. Freedom includes giving and receiving Love and attention wherever possible.

By realizing our parents to be bound within their own karmic cellular memories, we must assist them spiritually as much as they are willing, and we are able.

The only responsibility we have in truth to our family members is to honor their rights as individuals and allow them to have their own experiences. Very much work is needed by humanity in family relationships to free one another emotionally and mentally. By allowing each person close to us to have their own experiences and not interfering, we give them the opportunity to take full self responsibility, and the earlier in life a soul does this, the quicker they can hopefully grow in wisdom and strength. Love always wants the best for each person, and we must all feel that we always do our best, and give counsel when asked. That is my guideline.

Once again, it is through a revolution in conscious awakening that we will witness the enlightened state in all relationships.

NATURAL EASE OF LIVING

This is a fundamental technique in what I call "The Way of the Goddess." Living close with nature in pure environments shows one how to recognize nature as a valuable teacher and friend, and assists one in becoming sensitive to the finer vibrations of the Devic world and energy vortices. I have found this to be true in my life and it has therefore become an invaluable method which we share. Living with this natural ease in a quiet, beauty-filled, clean environment is very much The Way of the Goddess, and brings a great strength of peaceful reflection. We allow nature to assist us in the healing process with all who come our way. We mostly live close to oceans, rivers, lakes, mountains, and forests, and encourage daily communion with the Mother.

When we hold retreats to guide others we require a pure environment for people so they can heal in tune with the vitality of nature. Here they experience a pure reality that exists away from the dense, stressful cities.

The Mother also guides us to specific vortices where certain group soul karmas are held within the earth's karmic cellular layers (the inner earth ethers). We are shown the nature of these karmas,

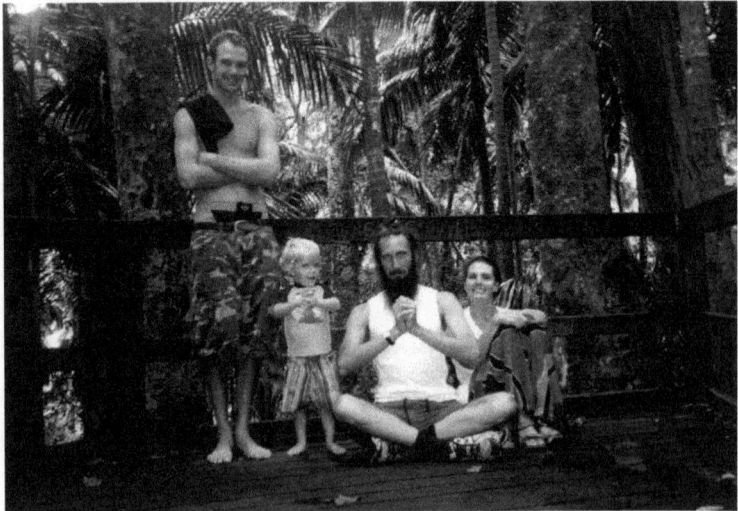

and the souls who are ready to release these limitations are drawn in to that area and into our safe conscious energy field, so they may understand and awaken more to the power of their "creations." This is a very total and pure way for empowerment to come directly to each person through the Mother's Grace, in alignment with each soul's timing. The timing for lifting of group karmas is ordained by the "ONENESS," it is already programmed into the inner ethers and is in no way a forcing or manipulation of the light.

By lying on the earth, swimming in pure cold waters, or walking or running in the forests and/or beaches, one becomes more able to feel their true nature, and can give all the hurts in a graceful way to the great Mother who nourishes all. By reflecting within the silence of nature a person is easily tuned to their inner state. If this state appears disturbed and noisy, one can surrender to nature as a means of relinquishing this disturbance.

Yes: surrender (alignment) is once again the key. Through the willingness to align, One takes on the very stillness of the Mother. Nature is never in a hurry!

This practice or method over time reveals a very natural ease of expression. People become more connected into their body temple, (their earth), and can feel the peace that they want all the time. It is our natural state to feel happy and at ease. Once established in this state a soul will never wish to enter into stressful struggling existence again. This is what I call transcending third dimensional karmas.

CRYSTAL HEALING

As mentioned earlier in the book, crystals are tools to repair and reconnect to the etheric body. Activation of the etheric body opens up a person's inner vision and vitality. When a person acknowledges self responsibility for spiritual growth, the next step is to be willing to see what our creations look like on every level, and to see how we really perceive ourselves in relation to others. We use the crystals as the physical medium in which to direct people's attention to their etheric imaging, to make what changes they want step by step. This is a valuable aspect of One's Sadhana, and is not to be confused with the superficial attraction of collecting crystals because they are in vogue. When One experiences a deeply revealing crystal healing there is a need to have a strong Sadhana to stabilize the effects of this healing and to be able to hold the changes that were initiated at the etheric level. If a person is not practising a transformative disciplined Sadhana they will vacillate in the energy, taking two steps forward and two steps back.

DREAM YOGA

It is recognized that mankind generally uses only one-tenth of the brain's full capacities. The underlying nine-tenths reside in the subconscious or unconscious spheres. The willingness to become all of who we are is the willingness to bring our subconscious and unconscious into awakened consciousness.

This, then, is the activation of the subconscious realms. Our main way of being able to tap into these inner realms is through remaining conscious during our sleep state. As a person applies dynamic techniques to awaken the Kundalini, one's conscious awareness extends into these realms more naturally. We consistently find that after people practise the teachings for a short period of time, they become a lot more conscious of the inner teachings coming through their dream activity.

The Universe always, always responds to our impulses. One is able to see what underlying issues are coming to the surface to be addressed and healed. Fifty percent of the healing of any issue is the bringing of the issue into the light to see its obviousness, and seeing how it creates limitation.

The more clear and conscious our daily state, the more clear and revealing our dream state. This is why we call it dream yoga. So much physical Karma that may otherwise occur in a dramatic physical event can be dealt with gracefully on the inner planes by seeing how we have created these limited tendencies, then rewriting the scripts and releasing any judgements from this level. We have personally witnessed the reality of this statement with ourselves and others on many occasions.

In dream Yoga we expand our consciousness to become consciously aware in both daytime and dream activity, moving into a continuum of consciousness. Thus we have defeated the illusion of death, and awakened into realization of our eternal existence as consciousness itself.

Dreams need to be understood on the level on which they occur. One either intuitively understands the implied meaning, or it is best to note them down, meditatively reflect upon them, and wait and see if a meaning comes into focus at a later date. There are a number of levels of dream activity. We call some of these *"inner transmissions,"* which occur from the formless Oneness and are profound blessings. There are also past hurts coming up for personal healing, and there is our connectivity in the collective psyche with collective healing involving small or large soul groups. These healings serve to further actualize one's potential future movement and occurrences. Much learning can be achieved in dream Yoga as we grow to honor and listen to the inner promptings of our Higher Self.

The environment in which you sleep plays an important part in the quality of dream yoga. We have found in cities there are psychic pollution and disharmonious thoughts which put a "dense" ceiling around one's auric field. Electrical lines also add confusion. Dream Yoga can be a valuable transcendental angelic experience far more regularly in natural, pure, vital environments.

Dreams are an important step in Self activation and healing, and should be acknowledged with a daily purification and Sadhana regime, including releasing negative old mind programs. As One gets clearer on the astral-emotional level, One is able to receive more frequently the higher teachings from the Oneness, and the visible instructions of the Ascended Masters.

DIET

Though diet is of itself not a technique, it is included here because it is of great assistance when applying spiritual principles in one's life. Without a healthy physical body a person is greatly limited in the ability to express the joy and bliss of our earth.

It is widely known nowadays that our diet affects our health, emotions, and quality of life.

Having been brought up eating meat, then changing to a vegetarian diet over twenty years ago and constantly addressing my food quality and quantity, gave me plenty of opportunity to see how my body has gradually become refined through diet. As the body and mind become more refined, one registers more instantly the effects of all vibrations. Food has a vibrational quality as well as physical effects. We find climate, emotions, and environment affect one's diet.

Being vegetarian is for us essential; physically, emotionally, and environmentally. Why kill when we have all food sources essential to health without the necessity to kill, which is another karma? Eating meat stimulates animalistic tendencies in humankind and is a great detriment. I believe humans were never designed to eat meat, and that eating meat continues to stifle the spiritual growth process.

We are unwilling to go into restaurants as the partaking of our food has become such a blessed activity. We enjoy eating alone or with one or two others. We do not miss social interaction in this way or any other. Blessing food is an important part of eating also.

Our bodies are happiest in sensitive clean environments, and in this atmosphere we find it is best to eat foods in season, grown in the area, organic, fresh, mostly uncooked, and simply combined. We like or recommend fruits, sprouted seeds, vegetables, soaked nuts, soy milk and tofu, wheat grass, organic rice, beans, and tahini. During the healing crises and healing processes, each person will go through years of detoxification. At different stages people will require different combinations and percentages of cooked versus raw foods. The body wisely tells us when it needs food and when it is not hungry. All we need to do is learn to listen intently to our body's wisdom, and gain the knowledge of the best foods for our body. Having a skilled naturopath's assistance at crucial times of transition in diet and growth is important and recommended.

The foods we eat are signs of how healthy our physical body is, how connected we are to our inner light, and how clear our emotions are. So although a person does not become enlightened just because they are eating pure foods, it is definitely an essential positive natural step in the enlightenment process.

SWEAT LODGES

Sweat Lodges are an ancient American Indian form of purification, still highly valued by all people who experience this practice. Sweat lodges are dome shaped buildings built right onto the earth, about four feet high, and usually built to seat anywhere from four to ten people. In the centre is a dug out pit that holds rocks that have been heated on an outdoor fire for a number of hours. These rocks are brought in to the lodge to provide the heat for one to sweat in.

These rituals are very sacred and can bring about great realignment with one's connection to the earth Mother. We have found them to give people an experience that nothing else can. They are healthy, fun, profound in the deeper effects that they can have, and they are an avenue for people to experience deep emotional release and purification. Additionally, they are a great way for people to feel a strong bonding with the earth and with others sharing the ritual of purification.

We like to have sweats on the new moon to consciously bring in new activations of oneSelf, and at the full moon as a time to give thanks for the completions that have occurred with the rising of the moon's cycle. There is always a lot of Grace and Love with the Mother to be enjoyed in these precious moments for everyone who participates, and we strongly recommend them to everyone.

A FEW KRIYA MEDITATIONS TO PRACTICE

Pranayam Up and Down Sides of Spine

This is a good preparatory breathing exercise to calm and center the mind, and increase the flow of soft energy in the body. As such, this practice prepares the mind and body to energetically support and surrender to deeper meditation and Kriya practice. It is excellent as an evening practice, dissolving tiredness from the day.

Block the right nostril by pressing against its side with your thumb. Inhale through left nostril, bringing the Prana and awareness down the left side of the spine to a count of eight. Hold the breath and circulate for a few moments at the base of spine. Exhale up the right side of the spine to a count of eight. Block the left nostril with your index finger and inhale through the right nostril down the right side of the spine to a count of eight, hold for few minutes at the base of the spine, and exhale up the left side of the spine to a count of eight. Continue for three to ten minutes.

Then relax the hands, and begin a new breathing discipline as follows. Inhale Prana and awareness up the spine. As you do so, feel that you are sucking the breath up within the spinal chord itself. Hold the breath and prana within the head for a few seconds, then slowly exhale it down the left side of the spine, all the way to the base, and hold your attention there for a few seconds with the breath held out. Inhale up the spine as previously mentioned, hold for a few seconds, and then slowly exhale down the right side of the spine. Alternating sides of the spine each time you exhale.

Continue this pattern for eleven to twenty-two minutes. During this time the mind is totally focused on the breath, and its subtle movement. If the mind wanders, bring it gently back. Wash through resistance with this breath, gaining clarity. This practice, while simple, must be done with your presence, and done long enough for the mind to switch into a new rhythm. Then the glands secrete in a new way, and meditation becomes automatic.

Pranayam for Sensitivity

Sit with a straight spine. Hold the hands in front of the solar plexus in fists, except for the index fingers which are straight. Hold the right palm facing down, and the left palm up. Cross the right index finger on top of the left index finger, crossing in the middle segment.

Inhale long and deep (about 15 seconds) through the nose. Exhale through puckered lips, directing the breath at the tips of the index fingers, taking about 15 seconds to exhale all the breath out. Feel a tingling at the fingertips. Yawning is an internalization of energy, keep up.

This Kriya is said to bring an intuitive sensitivity to minute changes in the "feel," or electromagnetic field of your environment. This may indicate weather, earthquake, mood changes of the area, etc. It increases the internal flow of energy and vitality, thus eliminating depression.

Practice for 11 minutes each day.

Sa Ta Na Ma Meditation

This Kriya has the capacity to balance all aspects of your creation in relation to the central viewpoint of your beingness. If you are too much out of your body, it will help to bring you in. If you are too stuck in the denseness of the body, it will help to expand you beyond the body. It is a meditation of creation, balance, simplicity, purification, and expansion.

It develops the ability to project and heal, bringing out what is called the Arcline projection. This projection, depicted as the halos around pictures of the saints, strengthens as the energies above the head (which exist beyond limited personality,) are grounded into the embodiment.

Developing the Arcline projection helps keep you cleansed of psychic vibrations, resulting in greater clarity of thought. You will have the capacity to choose how you receive thought, and according to your inclination, beam back a response. A strong Arcline projection is a sign of stability in the midst of constantly changing influence.

Sit in a meditative posture, with a straight spine.

Chant: **"Saa Taa Naa Maa"**

As you chant:

Saa - Press thumb and first finger together.

Taa - Press thumb and second finger together.

Naa - Press thumb and third finger together.

Maa - Press thumb and little finger together.

Sa Ta Na Ma

Chant in the following format of three voices:

5 Minutes Normal voice, The voice of creation

5 Minutes Whispering, A sense of longing, of lovers

11 Minutes Silent, of the Soul (chanting mentally and moving the fingers)

5 Minutes Whisper

5 Minutes Loud

---

31 Minutes : Total : which is a rhythm of mental atonement.

Eyes are one-tenth open, looking softly at the tip of the nose. This stimulates the third eye point. Feel as if the energy to press the fingers together originates from the navel point. Feel a continuous current of energy flowing in from above the head and into the body. If you hear the internal tones, then relate to it in this way, otherwise you can imagine it as a continuous "aaaa" sound. Most of the current enters the head, and then makes a ninety degree turn and exits through the forehead to infinity.

Place the sounds of the mantra on this current. As you hear the subtle tones, modulate them with the sounds of the chant. When this happens you will be listening to the chant as much as you are saying it.

Sometimes in meditation we go into deep spaces, and are not able to maintain consciousness of it as we return to physical sensory awareness. Switching through the different voices helps one in being able to integrate deeper experiences into daily consciousness awareness.

"Sat Naam" translates as "The God that I Am." Sat is truth (formless), and Naam is your essential identity in form. Broken down further:

Sa: The Infinite Ocean of Conscious potential.

Ta: Light of form at the third eye, Goddess energy, Yes.

Na: Purification and quickening of body-mind to receive the Divine current.

Ma: Manifestation, Birth, Mother.

This meditation tells the story of the formless consciousness creating light, the preparation for that light to be integrated into existing creation, and finally the joy of manifest creation.

Let the sounds wash the mind as the waves of the ocean wash the beach. Hidden patterns and thoughts will be brought up from the depths to be seen and released. Keep the purity of the chant continuous. If thoughts are playing loud in the mind, then play the mantra louder, by imagining millions of angels vibrating and singing the mantra with you, so the sound seems to emanate from all spaces. Let the sky speak it, and your body resound it. Remember to feel the navel as you touch each finger together.

Chapter Twenty Two

ATTAINING LIBERATION

*W*hat does it mean to be liberated? The Mother understands this very well. She sees everything as equally free. Our Mother allows everything to take its place in creation, then play out what is needed for its growth and understanding.

Very, very graciously the Mother watches and allows the souls who play on Her surface to experiment, incarnation after incarnation, until eventually realizing what this word Liberation truly means.

Liberation is attained as a result of realizing the True understanding: that we are, always have been, and will always be, totally Liberated. It is coming home! To be the Light of the One is Liberation, that is being our Divine birthright. It is individual will reborn into the Divine Will, then expressed in alignment (surrender) with the Divine (natural) laws.

To be an individual embodiment with the consciousness of at Onement is nothing less than perfect peace, bliss, and the joyous expression of God/Goddess playing through form.

In the illusion of separate existence, we become focused into structure and form. Again and again, we attempt to shape what Liberation looks like, and frequently create religions, systems, wars, philosophies, etc., to dictate liberation to others. These creations contract the uncontained Divine lifeforce which is flowing through form at all times. Thus the individual will becomes a distortion of the Higher Will, and is unable to acknowledge a soul's totality.

As a result of these actions, souls become caught in the illusion of duality and experience fear. Fear comes as a result of this separation, thus creating more and more illusions such as believing in ownership of the earth, planetary resources, and other people. In the illusion of separate identity, we imagine that we belong to a certain country, to a certain set of social cultural rules, to a certain religion, to a certain family, or to a certain partner. All of this is a contraction and a great limitation on truth. Many people know in their hearts the truth of this statement, yet very few have the burning desire or the internal voltage necessary to break free from all these self-imposed limitations.

LIBERATION IS HAPPINESS WITHOUT REASON. It is dependent on no external situation. It is not dependent on having to maintain any image, lifestyle, social face, or belief system. Liberation is the expression of natural uncontained lifeforce, which gives natural and what some may call supernatural abilities. Many times over the past six years My Beloved Virochana has demonstrated His happiness as a state which is dependent on no external situations. He remains happy even under what we may term adverse situations, and has shown me the fullness and power of this great truth.

Liberation must be regained if we are to become God/Goddess embodied on this Earth. The Mother silently demands that we surrender to who we are. This Earth is Her Bliss body, it is Her abode and every form is of Her Bliss, and everything of Her purity must be respected and acknowledged and attuned to. In this Oneness, Liberation is experienced. Liberation is also contained within the mystery of the Divine, therefore it eludes all description. This mystery cannot be understood by duality (the mind), it can only be appreciated, welcomed, and happily lived each moment, breathed with each breath, and held in gratitude and glory of each rising of the sun, and each flowering of a new flower. This is the gift we gave to our Self. This is the gift of life on earth.

The first step towards Liberation is the understanding of the true nature of all existence (One's true nature). This stage is what we call Clarity or Enlightenment. From here, there is no need to continue the struggle that exists within separative consciousness, no need to convert others out of insecurity, no need to create another set of rules for people to live by. Thus we find that enlightenment has no imposing external conditions and thus we become SELF REALIZED.

We are then free of all desires other than playing out the Will of The One, the Divine will. In this state we live happily, and simultaneously become the mystery in an uncontracted expression. We are embraced in the mystery knowing it as mastery each moment, and dance forth in that mastery our unique Divine expression.

TO EMBRACE LIFE FULLY IS TO EMBRACE DEATH, for here the individual "I" dies into the Self, or the Oneness contained in the totality of each moment. This is Liberation, it is that simple. The Mother wishes that we return to this, so we may experience True lasting Happiness. SAT NAAM WAHAY GURU! - Ecstatic is the all pervading form of God!

Liberation can also be expressed as a free state of being which arises from understanding our identity beyond all form, thereby breaking attachment to form and transcending Karma, which we have come to know as incomplete habitual activities. We have found that people easily become offended if we say that we are Liberated. It is a misconception that Liberation is something far out of reach of the ordinary person.

With the incoming higher frequency of the "New Age" we are now being given the tools and the freedom to redefine, reformat, and reprogram existing limitations. These include the limitations of old structures, old concepts of how we perceive our place in the Universe in Creation, and old languaging that perpetuates limited thought. Indeed those of us who have been blessedly exposed to some of this redefining find limited thought a prison for humankind.

Much of this redefining has come with the great assistance of the Extra Terrestrial energy via channels. The few I have experienced as being of great value in my own liberation process included Mafu and Ramtha (in the years preceding 1989) both of whom are Pleiadean Masters of the Oneness. Also Bashar, a wonderfully light and funny Master from Assasani, and Lazarus, a Masterful blending of the ONENESS. I highly recommend the tapes of these Masters to anyone seeking liberation.

In this reprogramming we are freeing old structures including the way "spirituality" has been held as some lofty achievement. Awakening has become first and foremost the taking back of the power we have given away. Willingness to take full responsibility for our own creation, and knowing we have the power to change our lives into anything which we see as bringing to us more happiness and joy of simply being!

This awakening process has also the fundamental understanding that we are LOVE and are totally supported by the Universe in being the free flow of energy which LOVE is.

With all this integrated fully into daily awareness, cemented with elevating practices and lifestyle, liberation becomes very accessible, and tangibly felt as real and ongoing.

We enjoy every step of this wonderful journey called life, and wish this same liberation for all our brothers and sisters.

Right here, right now we must be able to acknowledge ourself first as complete, worthy, and Divine, and acknowledge that Divinity is truly our most natural state. It is old programming created out of separative unenlightenment, that causes people to buy into guilt and sin, and feel a deep lack of Self worth.

My Beloved and I have realized the process of Liberation as a process of many embodiments culminating now in this Golden Age. For us the reality is that we have attained this level at a relatively young age in order to be of benefit on the planet. There are souls right now ripe for all karmic completions - through which they will achieve liberation so that we may collectively move forward to happier and greater manifestations on earth. We are here as Kumaras to assist the planetary Logos, the Ascended Masters, as an energy of the CENTRAL SUN. We are now with Grace able to assist our spiritual family from an uncontaminated level, so that the "Christed light" of each person may awaken in the quickest, purest possible way. We know there are many souls at this time ready for this completion. It is the planetary-ordained timing for this event. Those beings who are in process for the completion of their spiritual awakening, (which the Mother so urgently needs), will feel inspired by these words.

Having the Beloved at my side in daily relationship enables me to maintain this conscious state of Liberation in a very natural way. It is a great balancing as we are constantly there for each other. We feel blessed, for there is no reason to be anything else. For us Liberation is a state of most natural at easement with Self. We have seen the Divine working out in many situations, and therefore have nothing to struggle for, or to prove, as everything is perfect, and we play our small part in "perfecting the perfection." Many books on the lives of the Great Masters constantly refer to the very fact that these Masters were uncontrived, happy, at ease, unpredictable, and transcendent of the goings on around them. This is what we have gradually awoken into.

There is the added reality that until every soul on this planet is Liberated, a Liberated being feels the limited collective Liberation. For as long as there is the condition of unenlightenment on the planet, One who is no longer in a separative condition will automatically feel it, and be drawn into the activities of Awakened LOVE - serving, in a clear way, people wanting to be free and happy. Therefore One's activities remain to some degree in the arena of service. This service from the Liberated state has been written about in many scriptures and books as the great sacrifice of the Bodhisattvas. This is an example of the old languaging which feels contracted! We see it as a small sacrifice, but much more so, that it is a natural ongoing step of sharing Light. The whole idea of emphasizing sacrifice ignores the truth that service is simply the movement of Awakened Love.

Being liberated and living as the Beloved consciousness is such an ongoing, happy, all consuming state, that eventually everyone who comes in contact with this energy will be absorbed into this happiness. This is the transforming power of "LOVE."

Also Available From

BOOKS OF LIGHT

Sacred Mountain Retreat Center
PO Box 747
Crestone, CO 81131

---

www.sacredmountainretreat.org

Includes:
Upcoming Intensives, Planetary Journeys
Classes and Retreats at Sacred Mountain Retreat
The Tantric School of Meru and Aramu
Virochana and Shantara
Articles on Practice, the Ascended Masters, and Topics of
Interest
Books and Videos

This dynamic site is continually being updated and added to.

Sacred Mountain Retreat Center

Sacred Mountain Retreat Center is on 40 acres at the foot of the majestic Sangre de Christos Mountains in Southern Colorado. These mountains are alive in the same way as the Himalayas are potent. There is the residence of Virochana and Shantara, a beautiful meditation and practice dome, the yoga house (students practice house), self contained cabins, a fire circle, sweat lodge, and tipi. Also there are horses on the land, a greenhouse is planned and there are exquisite hiking trails from the retreat center itself.

The land was chosen by several Ascended Masters and is overseen by their ongoing activity. We are over 8,000 feet in elevation. Our water, from a deep well, is highly charged and healing.

This is a practice oriented place, and thus its primary service is in teaching the practices and helping those who are ready to awaken into the fullness of their being as self-realized radiant masters. In general, students come and live in the yoga house, where a daily morning and evening practice occurs, in addition to classes. Solitary retreats are also available.

Our approach emphasizes creation of a strong foundation. This includes dynamic yoga, meditation and kriya practice. Instruction and transmission is given in the Eternal Yoga and Tantric practices, from a long term perspective geared towards success. Every area of life is brought into consideration within this growth. For those who sincerely which to apply themselves, have a desire to be with their twin ray, to enter into a closer relationship with us and the Masters, all within the framework of their own mastery and participation in the bigger picture—then consider this invitation.

We travel regularly, teaching, and doing sacred work with the earth. Look at the web site to see our current teaching schedule, including upcoming intensives. If you would like to stay and practice within the yoga house, then send us an email, via the web site. Our tantric school and community is being expanded into New Zealand.

Virochana &
Shantara/MU

Tantra of the Beloved

by Virochana Khalsa
ISBN 0-9598048-9-7
600 pages $21.95

Finding Fulfillment in Life, Tantra, Emotions, Awakening a Body of Light, The Empowered Man and Woman, The Beloved Twin Ray, The Ascended Masters, Stellar Karmas, The Inner Earth and More...

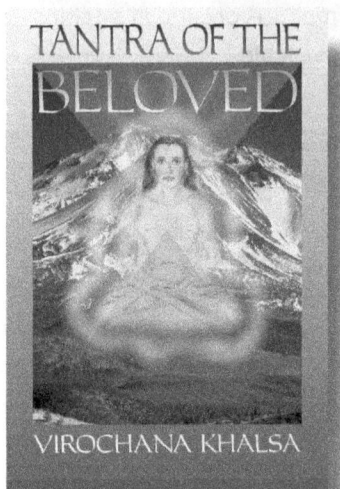

TANTRA OF THE
BELOVED

VIROCHANA KHALSA

"Spiritual growth burns the candle from both ends at once. From one end of the candle we face up to our limitations, see how they have served us and overcome them.

From the other end of the candle we acknowledge only our Eternal Perfection. All else is but shadows ignorantly cast by not seeing this Perfection. Eventually the shadow disappears and all is Light."

See additional quote on last page

Cultivating a Body of Nectar: Kriya Yoga and Tantric Foundations

by Virochana Khalsa
ISBN 1-929952-04-X
288 pages $21.95

Skillfully presented in this book are numerous methods to develop our blissful body of nectar.

After introducing an overview of the process, this well illustrated book includes an extensive section on meditative techniques known as kriyas.

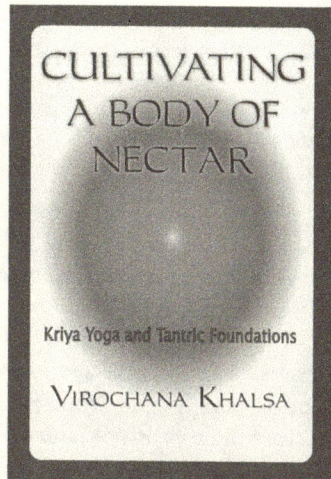

Virochana also explains, in his typical radiant wisdom, detailed understandings of chakras, channels, energy and essences through which we can create an inner temple.

"Through our blissful affair with cultivating nectar, we know our spirit in form...
Creating a body of nectar is an artful science that any of us can master through a steady, sincere and courageous application."

Tantra Unveiled, through the feminine

by Whitecloud Khalsa
ISBN 1-929952-03-1
144 pages $14.95

Tantra is a sacred doorway to the secret teachings, opened by mystics who embrace Divine Union.

The revelations and wisdom imparted in this book are from an experienced yogini. Whitecloud received the essence of Tantra from her first Master in India as a young woman, and has further developed this path with the assistance of numerous ascended Masters and her Twin-Ray.

This book is invaluable for anyone wanting to know the totality of what Tantra is as a spiritual path.

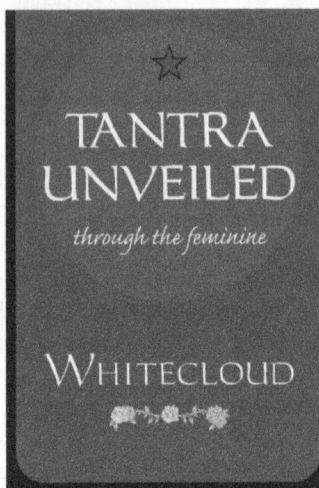

From the day I arrived my master drew me into his intimate radiance. He could make my fever rise and lower by the intensity of his attention towards me, all of which was on a non-verbal level. This force of love blissfully immobilized me. There were no questions within me; instinctively I knew my entire karmic residue was being purified in the fire of kundalini, all the dross being burned in the fever and I only knew love.

Resurrection of Earth and Human

by Whitecloud
ISBN 1-929952-07-4
68 pages $12.95

Our earth is an evolving living form. She is encoded with the capacity to cleanse away all that causes her disease. We the Human who have the ears to hear and courage to change must listen to her voice or we will not survive the coming changes. This booklet written at the request of the Ascended Masters Lord Meru and Mu, is for the Hu-man voices for change, voices for peace.

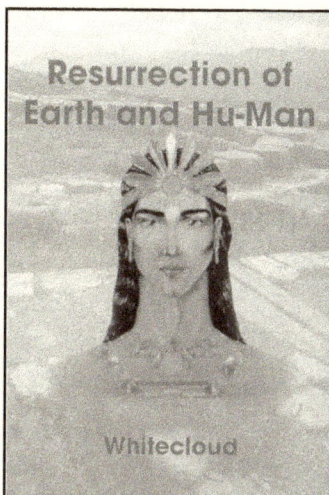

Resurrection of Earth and Hu-Man

Whitecloud

Coming Soon

Look on the web site www.sacredmountainretreat.org
for new books and videos.

"Non-dual nature is getting there by being there. For example, say you want clarification or guidance on some concern and go within for this purpose. If your mind is in a question mode, a "what if" mode, then you are open to all sorts of frequencies. Your mind could manufacture what you want to hear, or some influence in left field could say what it wants.

The non-dual approach is to first establish yourself in clarity, then expand your knowingness to understand the answer. Thus you first decree, "I AM Clarity." "I AM the clarity of whatever I want to know." However long it takes to establish this feeling, this alignment within yourself, is the inner work necessary to receive the knowingness of your answer.

In meditation practice, non-dual nature does not seek with the mind. In a chant, you are not trying to put together the meaning of the mantra, rather, you are deepening your vibratory presence with the mantra in a nonverbal centering. Yoga practice is thus a deepening of being there.

In non-dual nature you do not look to the techniques as your liberation, rather you simply use them to deepen your already known Presence. This simple understanding has very profound ramifications. Surprising as it may seem, many on the yogic path seem to miss it."

from Tantra of the Beloved - Virochana